Compliments of:

CENTER FOR LEARNING AND INNOVATION

LEARNING FOR LIFE

North Shore –
Long Island Jewish
Health System

LIJ

X-Engineering
the
Corporation

X-Engineering the Corporation

Reinventing Your Business in the Digital Age

JAMES CHAMPY

Published by Warner Books

An AOL Time Warner Company

Warner Business Books are published by Warner Books, Inc.,
1271 Avenue of the Americas, New York, NY 10020.

Visit our Web site at www.twbookmark.com

An AOL Time Warner Company

Printed in the United States of America
First printing: February 2002
10 9   8   7   6   5   4   3   2   1

Library of Congress Cataloging-in-Publication Data

Champy, James
        X-engineering the corporation : reinventing your business in the
    digital age / James Champy.
            p. cm.
        Includes index.
        ISBN 0-446-52800-5
        1. Reengineering (Management) 2. Business communication—Com-
    puter networks. 3. Business networks. 4. Customer relations. I. Title:
    Reinventing your business in the digital age. II. Title: Xengineering the
    corporation. III. Title.

    HD58.87 .C427 2001
    658.4'063—dc21

                                                        2001046847
                                                                CIP

Book design by Elliott Beard

To all my teachers,
in work and life

Contents

Contents

Chapter 1

Why X-Engineering? Why Now?

When Michael Hammer and I conceived our 1993 bestseller, *Reengineering the Corporation,* we recognized that the economy confronted a period of enormous change and that businesses urgently needed ways to respond. On all sides, companies were beset by globalization, by the sudden invasions of once-safe markets, by the growing demands of ever more sophisticated customers. All too many were strangling in departmentalization, mired in their single-minded focus on individual tasks. Our message: Work would have to be redesigned—reengineered, we called it—in terms of processes rather than tasks or departments.

The book touched a nerve, setting off a great wave of reengineering in company after company around the world. True to our vision, reengineering achieved enormous efficiencies. For example, a recent Massachusetts Institute of Technology (MIT) study, found that reengineering in the aerospace industry has led to a 30 percent boost in productivity since 1993. Similar productivity gains were reported in industries ranging from insurance to computer component manufacturing.

The impact of reengineering, however, was internal; by and large, the reforms ended at the company gate. That is no longer enough. The technology revolution and the global economic realignment of the past five years demand that businesses prepare for the next stage of transformation. The advances of reengineering must be extended to include all stakeholders—not just a company's shareholders, but its managers, employees, customers, suppliers, and partners as well.

I have heard much criticism that the efficiencies created by the first round of reengineering mainly benefited shareholders at the expense of customers and employees. As banks merged, for example, staffs were consolidated and downsized in the name of reengineering. Fewer people were asked to do more work, while others were laid off and customer service deteriorated. That imbalance cannot be sustained. Indeed, shareholders can expect to go on profiting from business changes only if—a crucial *if*—customers and employees begin to benefit as well.

What the world's harsh new economic conditions teach us, above all, is that every part of business is now connected at some level to every other part. All are interdependent. No part can thrive in isolation. Like the human body, the whole is healthy only if the parts are healthy.

This book was written to help managers confront the new challenge of connectedness and interdependency. Where reengineering showed managers how to organize work around processes inside a company, X-engineering argues that the company must now extend its processes outside—hence the *X,* which stands for crossing boundaries between organizations. When an organization's processes are integrated with those of other companies, all the partners can pool their efforts and effectively become a new multi-company enterprise, far stronger than its individual members could ever be on their own.

X-engineering is the art and science of using technology-enabled processes to connect businesses with other businesses and companies with their customers to achieve dramatic improvements in efficiency and create value for everyone involved.

What is driving this sweeping change is a combination of global competitive pressure and the frustrating inefficiency and redundancy that still persists in work relationships between organizations and with customers. The change is enabled, of course, by that all-purpose information medium, the ubiquitous Internet, and its associated technologies. When I call my approach X-engineering, I mean to invoke boundary-crossing on a scale approaching the Internet's ability to connect the world in a seamless web of transactions. This is hardly far-fetched. Many large organizations have already adopted forms of X-engineering, in practice if not yet in name.

Most businesspeople, I suspect, think of the reengineering movement as a thing of the past. I think it has just begun. X-engineering is reengineering *squared*: a vastly expanded new version, redesigned and refitted for timely service in the world's tough new business climate. With all due immodesty, I predict that the corporate transformations spurred by X-engineering in this decade will dwarf those wrought by reengineering in the last one.

Reengineering and X-engineering are alike in that they both make it possible to greatly improve business performance. They both require radical rethinking and fundamental change, and they both have a process focus. Then they part company. Reengineering is applied within the organization largely to cut costs, raise quality, and increase speed and productivity. X-engineering also improves internal efficiency, but that is just the beginning. It promises vast improvement in operations and processes across organizations—that is, among companies and their suppliers, partners, and customers. The result will be breakthrough innovations in the ways companies operate and new value propositions for customers. Ultimately, the X-engineered corporation mobilizes not only its own improved processes but also those of its X-engineered allies.

The potential impact of X-engineering can be glimpsed in this simple fact: Business spends about $2 trillion a year on logistics, 40 percent of which goes for paperwork and administration. X-engineering those processes could achieve mammoth savings. Right now, for example, the routine process of shipping something across the Atlantic is a logistical nightmare, thanks to red tape that requires shippers to execute 26 separate documents. If X-engineering could slash these administrative costs by half—a relatively modest ambition—companies and presumably consumers would be richer by $400 billion a year.

In the chapters ahead, I set forth in detail the theory and practice of X-engineering. I also offer case histories of some of the businesses that have made great strides by applying X-engineering concepts. In this chapter, my goal is more modest. I show how reengineering and X-engineering were born. I explain why the business world has been so slow to adapt to the Internet despite its huge potential, and I detail how this new technology is changing the very definition of the corporation.

From Reengineering to X-Engineering

One of our key insights into the need for reengineering came from an insurance executive who sought our help in the late 1980s. He told us that it took his company 24 days to issue a new policy—nearly a month just to write up a simple life policy and send out a bill. The delays were both annoying and expensive, but that wasn't the worst of it. "Here's my real problem," he said. "I don't want to give reluctant customers that much time to change their minds."

It turned out that the actual time necessary to create and print a policy and send a bill was 10 minutes: After all, policies are usually composed of standard boilerplate clauses, and every department was fully automated. So how could the process conceivably take 24 days?

We traced the order's paper trail through the organization. We visited the 14 different departments on its route. We saw all the computers—and we concluded that the company's problem was caused by its extreme fragmentation and specialization. No amount of increased efficiency inside those 14 separate stovepipes was going to help. The only way to make any dramatic gain in our client's performance was to tear down the system, dismantle those stovepipes, and create a clear, clean line from the beginning to the end of every process.

And that became reengineering.

A decade later, in the summer of 2000, I had a similar epiphany about X-engineering. It came while I was sitting in the conference room of Harvard Pilgrim Health Care, Inc., a health maintenance organization (HMO) in Boston, Massachusetts. Founded by a group of doctors from Harvard Medical School and previously known as Harvard Community Health Plan, it has always been committed to providing the best possible health care.

Harvard Pilgrim had a new chief executive officer, Charles D. Baker, who had arrived to find impending disaster. At least $100 million of previously unreported red ink was on the books, and there wasn't much of a cushion to lean on. Even more disturbing, the organization, like many HMOs, was having trouble tracking its expenses and its members.

Baker's questions were initially about survival. How does a business get into a condition where it learns about its real income and costs a full year after it closes its books? How could it fix its operations and get its financials under control while continuing to provide the quality health care that had made its reputation?

Baker and his new management team could have cut costs in the disturbing fashion of many HMOs—by simply dumping whole categories of patients who required more care than the norm. But these doctors and managers had a great sense of purpose: Not only did they want to use the best of their ability to continue to serve all their members, but they were going to solve all the conundrums that plague the health care industry.

Baker and his colleagues had other questions in need of answers: How can we improve our services, for example by tracking the outcomes of our treatments, without increasing the costs of health care? Why does it sometimes take over a year to settle up our financial arrangements with our doctors and hospitals? Why do our members have to fill out new forms and register again every time they see a new care provider? Why can't we have universal health care records, accessible to all providers—with the members' permission, of course? Why are all of us in health care spending as much as 35 percent of every expense dollar on administrative processes that often involve multiple health care providers and other insurers? What if we could spend most of that money directly on the delivery of care?

What struck me at our meeting was that a solution for Harvard Pilgrim would require more than reengineering the processes inside the organization. Harvard Pilgrim was not a finite business that could ever thrive alone, no matter how superb its internal processes might become. Like so many other businesses today, this HMO was essentially an intermediary, trading in information with its partners. It was, in fact, a complex network of mutual processes and relationships with other organizations.

Solving Harvard Pilgrim's problems would thus require crossing the boundaries of multiple organizations. The HMO would have to redesign its working relationships with members, employers, doctors, hospitals, and other insurers. Each player in the health care industry would have to change the way it added value to the patient's experience. And none of them could do it alone. The solution would require cross-organizational process change, shifts in strategy, and the generous application of the Internet and related information technologies. In the end, the health care industry would have to be reinvented. And the key to that kind of reinvention is what became X-engineering.

As I realized that day in Boston, there must be a broader approach to doing business that expands the application of technological advances across whole industries without respect to organizational or geographic boundaries. What had been vacuous concepts—"the networked economy" or the "virtual corporation," for example—could now be made a reality. But it would not happen simply through the application of technology. It would happen only if managers radically changed their business processes—this time not just within their companies or even just where customers and companies meet. The opportunity was now to create a new generation of processes that would cross the boundaries of organizations and be shared first between companies and eventually throughout a whole industry.

These new processes would both dramatically improve the performance of companies and the value they deliver to customers. I also realized that understanding the real effects of the Internet and the role of information technology would be critical to successful X-engineering. For example, I needed to decide whether these tools were disruptive or indispensable or perhaps both. After all, many company processes can and have been reengineered without the use of information technology. But in X-engineering the Internet is the central nervous system, the medium for sharing vital information and integrating disparate companies and their processes. It is indispensable to X-engineering. Not surprisingly, the Internet also brings all the challenges of disruption.

X-Engineering the Corporation

The power of the Internet as a technological development ranks with the advent of electricity, the internal-combustion engine, nuclear power, and the computer itself. It is the ubiquitous network that can link all organizations, and it is driving a fundamental shift in the way organizations operate. Over time, it will not only improve the performance of managers and employees—it will alter the very nature of their work. Moreover, it will allow organizations to become not just tools of change but creators of change.

Information has always been powerful; the Internet makes it very nearly omnipotent. We can now gather, analyze, and share information with a speed and sophistication that dramatically raises organizational intelligence. In our new digital democracy, what used to be "secrets" that managers believed provided competitive advantage become common knowledge almost instantly—information that farsighted companies disseminate to all hands. Transparency of information and processes becomes the norm.

This openness and ease of information dispersal is the key to mobilizing a company and its customers, suppliers, and partners for a common purpose. And that will enable almost miraculous efficiency. Every day, process-savvy companies use the Internet to routinely exceed performance levels unimagined 10 years ago. Just as the four-minute mile seemed impossible until Roger Bannister ran it one day in 1954—whereupon runner after runner matched his breakthrough until that milestone became routine—the performance standards of a decade ago are now easily surpassed.

There is a popular misconception that the breaking of the dot-com bubble on Wall Street signaled a disenchantment with the Internet as a way of doing business and even with high technology in general. Not so. What has changed is how technology and the Web are being used. At the retailer Staples, Inc., for instance, even as management slammed the brakes on launching new e-businesses and folded its Staples.com subsidiary back into the parent company, new technology was being put in place to increase efficiency. An investment of $2.5 million in a new data-storage system was expected to return $10 million in savings, and an online help desk for store managers and clerks should bring a 60 percent return on investment over four years—well over four times the average Staples return.

That is typical of the bottom-line savings we are seeing through process change and the application of technology. Here are some other examples:

- Item: FedEx Corporation is encouraging its customers to keep tabs on packages via its Web site. Why? It costs FedEx $2.14 to track a package if a customer calls its phone center, 4 cents if a customer does it via the Web. And FedEx receives more than 600,000 such queries a day.

- Item: By using online auctions, the pharmaceutical and consumer-products giant Bristol-Myers Squibb Company has trimmed 6 to 8 percent of its cost on everything from chemicals to medicine dispensers and reduced time in its purchasing process.

- Item: The health care provider Humana, Inc., used to spend $128 to handle a single job application and résumé. Putting that process online has collapsed the cost to a nearly invisible 6 cents, boosting productivity some 2,133 times.

- Item: Banks enjoy a savings bonanza when their customers use the Web. At one financial institution I know, the cost of handling a transaction over the Internet costs the bank just 2 cents, compared with 24 cents via a cash machine, 54 cents by telephone, and $1.25 by teller.

- Item: The General Electric Company is saving some $600 million a year. How? By making just a third of its procurement purchases online.

- Item: International Business Machines Corporation (IBM) has seen its purchasing costs drop by $6.5 billion in two years simply by putting its procurement process online. Another benefit of its e-procurement process: Its contract cycle time has declined from one year to 30 days.

In truth, the real potential of the Internet was never in auctions of gewgaws or the spamming of e-mail advertising. Cutting costs is the name of the Internet game. To be sure, investment in technology is turning down as companies digest the huge investments they have made in recent years. In a survey in May 2001, 260 chief information officers said their planned growth in technology budgets was down to 4 percent from 19 percent six months previously. But the plan was still to grow, and 70 percent of the respondents to a survey of 150 senior executives by the Wharton School of the University of Pennsylvania said Internet technology was crucial—both for customer service and for making purchasing more efficient.

Beyond all this, the Internet is transforming competition itself. Traditionally, companies have used various methods to capture and retain customers, improve operational efficiency, and achieve competitive advantage. In my consulting work I identified many of those options long ago. For example, companies have always sought to gain new efficiencies by trimming manufacturing costs, cutting inventories, and slashing distribution expenses. All that is still possible, but the use of the Internet will lift all boats. Competitors' costs will become similar—and their prices will drift closer together.

This leveling of the playing field is being accelerated by a wave of new alliances and partnerships. Ronald Coase, the Nobel Prize–winning economist, pointed out years ago that the high transaction costs involved in finding and working with new partners led companies to try to do everything themselves. Today the Internet has made partnering easier and far less expensive. This has encouraged many businesses to look outside their borders, seeking alliances with companies that can perform particular processes better than they can. Paradoxically, the nature of competition today leads companies to cooperate. In other words, the right conditions are in place for X-engineering

It is abundantly clear that information technology has become the 600-pound gorilla in thousands of businesses the world over. The task for managers is to master the new technology instead of becoming its victim.

Fear and Longing

Fear of the new, longing for the old, all muddled by a desire not to fail—such are the emotions that confuse high-tech novices in any industry, and especially in those confronting X-engineering for the first time. This is nothing new. Progress has exacted a price in perceived danger ever since the first labor-saving loom scared English textile workers into torching their mills. The price of today's technology is clear: Understand its business impact or fall behind, perhaps forever. Accordingly, every manager now realizes that sooner or later he or she will have to accept and adopt the Internet. But the technology is advancing so rapidly that many find themselves nearly overwhelmed by the possibilities. Buried in information, with too little time to absorb and apply it, these managers grope along from day to day in a fog of unanswered questions:

- The Internet is vital to my company's future, but how can I use it? I have already downsized, right-sized, reinvented, restructured, and, yes, reengineered. What else can I squeeze out of the business and my workforce?

- How do I know I'm making the right technology choices? How do I keep up with the constant and rapid evolution of technical products? Where am I supposed to get the money?

- How much of this technology should I develop for myself, and how much can I leave to partners? How much control of my operations can I afford to give up to suppliers and partners?

- If the "networked economy" means getting closer to my customers and suppliers, how can I exert control over my business? Can I still run my business the way I want to? Who's in charge?

- How long can I put off major decisions about changing how I operate? And most troubling of all, why should I change and embrace technology when the Internet seems to do nothing but drive down the price of my products?

The answers to these questions and many similar ones will be found in the chapters ahead, but this much can be said right now: In the real world, a company's decisions about business change that is driven or enabled by new technologies often owe less to logic than to long-established patterns of managerial behavior.

Although managers recognize that the Internet and other technologies will affect their businesses, they aren't sure how, and that uncertainty breeds anxiety. They have only a flimsy grasp of the Internet's possibilities and the operating changes it will demand. Accordingly, they respond with nothing more venturesome than brochure-ware—pro forma, this-is-who-we-are Web sites. Danny Hillis, the legendary cofounder of Thinking Machines Corporation, pointed out a common failing in a recent speech at the Santa Fe Institute:

> All companies think of e-commerce as an add-on to their existing business. I call this the drive-in window mistake. When cars first came along, many businesses just assumed that they would add a drive-in window but that the rest of their business would essentially remain the same. [But] the real impact of cars was to move shopping traffic from downtown to the shopping malls. Suddenly, realize it or not, everyone was in the shopping-by-car economy. In the same way, all business is becoming e-commerce. Adding a Web portal to your existing business is like adding a drive-in window to a downtown department store. Instead, information drives the entire process from discovering products to selecting them, transporting them, servicing them, and managing the relationship with the customer. Managers must rethink their entire business.

Many managers choose to disregard Hillis's advice. They remain skeptics, understandably turned off by Web evangelists who spout overwrought prophecies ("be digital or die"). The recent crash of dot-com companies is also cited as a good reason to put off technology initiatives or experiments with new ways of doing business. To be sure, the debacle was real, but the collapse of a Wall Street bubble must not be confused with the enduring technology that inspired investors to inflate that bubble and that will undoubtedly outlive it.

I have met other company leaders who react to the Internet with what I call the not-on-my-watch response. They know or suspect the potential impact of the new technology, but they choose to do nothing about it. They draw denial about their shoulders like a comforting cloak, assuring themselves and their colleagues that nothing major needs to be done for another decade or two.

Five years ago, for example, the executives of a major Southern bank visited me in my office in Cambridge, Massachusetts. They wanted to talk about the future of retail banking. We spent the morning discussing this, and around noon I told my visitors that I was going to give them a glimpse of their future—a demonstration of what a virtual, digital bank looked like. I brought out my laptop and pulled up the site of a British bank that had just gone online.

As the bankers witnessed what services were available and how quickly and easily transactions could be completed, the conversation began to wander. A strange levity filled the room. One man turned to me and said, "Jim, tell me, do we have to fly home in our own plane or are you going to beam us home?"

I could see that my Southern friends were not really up for any more talk about the Internet's impact on their lives and livelihoods. They chose to shrug it off. It might be true that some day the Internet would cause their massive infrastructure of branch banks to crumble, forcing them to fire or retrain thousands of people. But surely it wouldn't happen on their watch.

Eventually, I realized that the unstated reasons why people avoid new technologies are neither simple nor perverse. Indeed, it is human nature to be uncomfortable with the very notion of major change. As Shakespeare's Hamlet put it, we would all "rather bear those ills we have/Than fly to others that we know not of."

Hamlet preferred denial to dread. So do most people. Unless you are dead certain that change will be beneficial, unless you have an unusual degree of courage and sureness in your judgments, you are likely to make one of two choices when confronted by a potentially transforming new technology. Neither response will allow your company to advance.

The first choice is Hamlet's: to dither and ultimately do nothing. The second is to do something small. Most managers have been taught to take an incremental approach to change. Small actions rarely lead to large mistakes. We can easily backtrack. We can defend our actions to our directors and the market. Yes, we can say, we know all about the Internet, and we are moving gradually and prudently in response.

In truth, however, incremental change is fruitless when it comes to embracing a technology that by definition creates radical business change. And even if small steps were useful, as I learned to my dismay while helping businesses reengineer in the 1990s, every large organization has the corporate antibodies to kill any incremental change program.

More than 30 years ago, the U.S. Congress established the Office of Technology Assessment precisely to evaluate the secondary effects of new technologies, including their disturbance of traditional ways of life and business. It turned out to be an almost impossible task. Trying to predict the ripple effects of a new technology is a dubious proposition. In our hubris, we can make grand pronouncements—but in our wisdom we must realize that they are, at best, educated guesses.

The history of Thomas Edison's invention of the electric light is instructive. It turned out to be far more than simply a convenience, an alternative to high-cost manufactured gas. The rhythms and very nature of our lives were forever altered. The lightbulb opened up the night: We could read at all hours, work longer days, party 'til dawn. (At the same time, we learned to get along on less sleep—20 percent less than our counterparts of a century ago, according to the National Sleep Foundation.)

Could any of this have been envisioned by the businesspeople of Edison's day? Unlikely. Edison made his discovery in 1879, but as the economic historian Paul David points out, it took 40 years or so before the nation woke up to the real potential of electricity.

15

Manufacturers, for example, could not see any particular advantage in the new power source. They were doing quite well, thank you, with their basement steam engines sending power upstairs via belts and pulleys to run factories four or five stories tall. Switching from steam to electricity seemed at first to offer no visible gain. It was not until the manufacturers came up with a new vision of their factories that the modern, one-story plant emerged, with each machine run by its own motor.

Arguably, there was plenty of time to digest changes in those days. But today innovations occur at unprecedented speeds, and reaction time has shrunk to what seems like nanoseconds. This creates more confusion and anxiety for managers. How do we understand and capitalize on a new technology before the next best thing overtakes it? And can a company ever be entirely sure that it has chosen the right course when it makes a radical change in its operations?

With X-engineering the fear and longing will be about a lot more than technology. Managers will be pressured to surrender hard-won control to the greater good of business-to-business and business-to-customer integration—to literally share their entire companies with other companies and customers. To some leaders this will feel reckless, a form of managerial abdication. Your reactions will be shaped by years of competitive behavior:

- Do I really want to trust my company's intimate secrets to strangers who may have only their own interests at heart? Are my partners and customers hiding their real agendas?

- My people and I spent our whole lives honing our competitive instincts—that is how we built this great company and that is what keeps it great. Frankly, we are trained warriors and proud of it. Okay, I understand that we now have to turn our guns into plowshares and all become peaceful X-engineers. I know it intellectually. But it is jarring to my sensibilities.

- Everyone in my business can tell you the stories of mergers and acquisitions that failed because of incompatible cultures and leaders. Won't this be a problem in X-engineering? After all, we are unique and indubitably superior to the others. How can we avoid oil-and-water conflicts and an early divorce? Failed mergers typically squander millions on visions that never should have been pursued, much less articulated. Tell me how our X-engineered vision can escape that fate and instead thrive for the common good.

Acknowledging our denials and our fears is the first step to overcoming them. It is also the first step every manager must take on the road to X-engineering. Then, as with any set of new ideas, it is important to understand how they apply to your business. And you will learn how to do that in the next chapter.

Chapter 2

What X-Engineering Is—and Isn't

In the early 1900s The General Electric Company was experiencing problems with one of the huge generators it manufactured at the company's plant in Schenectady, New York. When no one could figure out how to fix it, GE called in the great electrical engineer Charles Proteus Steinmetz, who duly spent several days examining the machine and all its drawings. After he departed, GE engineers found a large "X" chalked on the generator casing. A note from Steinmetz instructed them to cut the casing open at that spot and remove so many turns of wire from the stator. The generator would then work—and so it did.

Asked to name his fee, Steinmetz pondered and eventually proposed a then-immense number—$1,000. Stunned, GE's bean counters requested a detailed invoice justifying the charge. When it arrived, it consisted of two items:

1. Marking chalk "X" on the side of generator: $1

2. Knowing where to mark chalk "X": $999

For X-engineers, as for Steinmetz, the required skill is knowing where to put the *X*—where to cross boundaries, where to redesign processes, where to achieve what benefit and with whom. As with Steinmetz, *X* marks the spot where intuition joins technique and solutions emerge.

In the preceding chapter I argued that X-engineering is a critical business imperative for the twenty-first century. In this chapter I review its major components and begin explaining how you can put it to work.

To give you a flavor of X-engineering in practice, let's first examine Chicago-based R. R. Donnelley & Sons Company, one of the largest printers in the United States. Like some other companies that I will examine, Donnelley has embraced X-engineering's core idea—process change across organizations—without, in fact, having ever heard of something called X-engineering. I offer that fact as evidence that X-engineering is not an academic notion but a natural response to today's economic realities. Donnelley's transformation is certainly a case of doing what comes naturally.

Donnelley prints books, magazines, catalogs, directories, inserts, brochures—just about anything that can be printed. Its primary customers are publishers of every ilk, including the giant media company AOL Time Warner, Inc. Its primary suppliers are paper mills.

As a paper-bound business, Donnelley was directly threatened by the Internet and its much predicted effect, the paperless society. Fortunately for Donnelley, the world has not yet stopped devouring the printed word. But there is a serious threat to Donnelley as media and catalog companies put some of the profits from their print enterprises into building their Internet presence.

Every dollar they spend on their electronic channels is a dollar not spent on printing.

The Internet also figures in another trend that threatens Donnelley and its suppliers. The big general-interest magazines, such as *Reader's Digest*, that have long been the mainstay of non-book printing, are faltering. Large media companies are now segmenting their print products into highly defined vertical niche markets, selling not simply to women, for example, but to "women between 45 and 60 years of age who have significant disposable income and a garden." And these same media companies are increasingly using channels other than print to market their content. Martha Stewart, once confined to books and magazines, now shows up on television promoting her Web site.

In a recent speech, William L. Davis, chairman, chief executive officer, and president of Donnelley, acknowledged the impact of the Internet in talks with his suppliers, but he urged that it be viewed as inspiration rather than impediment. "I am convinced," he said, "that the Web is an opportunity . . . for printers, paper manufacturers, and content owners to create a new kind of relationship based on a win/win/win proposition."

Davis said he intended to transform his company: "We will no longer be thought of as strictly print-and-bind. We will be seen as an integrated communications solutions provider."

Donnelley understood that if it wanted to keep its customers, it was going to have to make the paper-and-printing function as problem-free and cost-effective as possible. It also realized that the Internet itself offered the most effective response Donnelley could make to the very threat the Internet posed. The company set about redesigning its processes in partnership with the paper mills.

Step one focused on process. Donnelley's managers presided over a single continuous process that started with the forest, ran through the mills, the printing plants, content, logistics, and ended up at the newsstand or in the mailbox. Under close scrutiny, it became clear that the supply chain needed work. Price levels for paper were unstable. Inventory levels fluctuated, indicating that there was too much cash tied up in storage that might have been used for other, more critical business needs. There was little or no integration among the members of the supply chain, a formula for operational inefficiency.

What was needed, the company decided, was a new partnership with the paper suppliers to reduce waste, lower inventory, improve cycle times and flexibility, continuously innovate, and relentlessly address the total delivered cost of the customer's product—from the forest to the front door.

Then Donnelley brought the customers themselves into the equation and set out to create the collaborative relationship described by Davis. To make that happen, the company has established fully integrated online linkages between its presses, its suppliers' paper machines, and the publishers they both serve.

Internally, Donnelley has been focusing on getting its pressrooms to run within predictable control parameters. When the pressroom is under control, paper manufacturers can experiment with their parameters and measure how their product performs. Executives at one paper supplier told Donnelley that having a controlled pressroom is like having a big laboratory at their disposal. Additionally, Donnelley and its suppliers are working to eliminate every redundant step in their processes.

Inventory management is a good example of this joint effort. Inventory presents an enormous challenge in the paper and printing industries. Traditionally, each publisher buys its own paper, conforming to its specifications and the page size of its publications. The price of paper fluctuates widely in response to demand, but if one of Donnelley's customers makes a large paper buy in anticipation of an imminent price hike, that company ties up a great deal of capital that could be better used elsewhere. Donnelley found itself caught in the middle of this dilemma, with the added inconvenience of being the storage facility for vast amounts of this inventory.

On any given day in Donnelley's plants, customers may have an average 60-day paper supply on hand. That is 298,000 tons of paper occupying space and doing nothing, paper worth $270 million. Most customers turn their inventory only six times a year. Boosting the number of inventory turns by 50 percent—to just nine times a year, which is by no means world-class—would free up $135 million in working capital for customers.

Publishers see huge inventories as insurance. They are terrified of being caught short, and they traditionally have little confidence in the ability of paper companies and printers to coordinate their orders and schedules. Donnelley is working to turn that attitude around.

Donnelly's solution to this puzzle was a model for this book. In my terms, Donnelly has X-engineered its customers' and suppliers' ordering and scheduling processes, together with its own, to produce a seamless flow of information and materials. It also got its own house in order by reengineering its pressroom processes.

Donnelley calls its effort Cooperative Paper Management. Donnelly takes the lead in coordinating paper orders with inventories and scheduled print runs. All three parties—publishers, paper mills, and Donnelley—have agreed to the new business processes. They all have discarded their artificial secrecy and opened their processes to provide the information required to achieve higher inventory turns. The Internet has made this possible. Paper deliveries have been accelerated and supplies stabilized, convincing publishers that hoarding is foolish as well as needless. The constant online information flow means that all three parties are on the same page with every job and project, and remain flexible and proactive. Inventory, delivery, and responsiveness to schedule changes, such as large last-minute print runs, have all improved exponentially.

As we can see from the Donnelley example, X-engineering, in simple terms, is about achieving breakthrough business performance by applying information technology to redesign processes that cross organizational boundaries. But it isn't easy. X-engineering doesn't come in a box for quick assembly. It tests your powers of analysis, imagination, and execution. Once understood, though, it can be used to address the enormous inefficiencies and redundancies in the work between companies and from there, create major opportunities and breakthrough efficiencies and advantages.

X-engineering requires that you rethink your whole business and all its relationships, not just with customers but also with suppliers, partners, employees—even competitors. It is broad in scope, encompassing both strategy and operations. It can't be delegated by executives to managers, and then by managers to employees. It requires attention to detail from all parties—yes, even the chief executive. It will intellectually challenge all participants, and its course can't be fully prescribed, or even foreseen. Also, its execution will require extraordinary managerial skill and discipline.

X-engineering responds to three business questions: How must a company now change? for what benefit? and with whose collaboration? The answers derive from close attention to three areas:

1. A company's processes, meaning all the things it does to create and sell its goods or services. This includes all the processes involved in its necessary business dealings with external players, among them customers, suppliers, distributors, partners, and shareholders.

2. The business proposition it offers its customers.

3. The extent of its participation with others in creating shared processes.

The Three Ps—process, proposition, and participation—form what I call the X-engineering triangle. The triangle encompasses some familiar company practices that are reinvented by X-engineering. For example, issues of strategy, operations, and relationships will merge and must be considered simultaneously. Managers will have to think more broadly about processes—within their own companies and beyond. No longer is a process strictly internal. It must be seen as one part of a multiorganizational whole. This calls for a new credo of cooperation. As in Donnelley's case, the orchestration of cross-organizational change requires unprecedented openness and collaboration between companies.

Now, let's consider each one of the Three Ps.

Process

In the late 1980s globalization and newly empowered customers put business processes under enormous pressure. It was the need to redesign those processes that inspired *Reengineering the Corporation*. At the time, I viewed processes as one of the central elements of a company, along with its people, structure, and strategy. I now see companies in a much larger perspective—not just as individual producers of goods and services but as combinations of processes. These processes interact with each other and with the processes of other organizations.

I understand that this view of the corporation is a radical departure, not just from my own previous perception but also from the generally accepted dogma as to the fundamental nature of the business organization. To be sure, people, structure, and strategy are still important, but their importance lies in their roles in the full complement of processes that determine, in the long run, the value of a company. Participants in this collection of processes include not only your company but also its customers, suppliers, distributors, partners, and competitors. You all need each other to do business. No one can do everything on their own anymore.

X-engineering, then, gives process a whole new dimension. Traditionally, processes have been viewed as proprietary, kept secret to create advantage the way The Coca-Cola Company guards its syrup formula or Tricon Global Restaurants, Inc., protects its Kentucky Fried Chicken batter recipe. If you told the world what you were doing, conventional wisdom held, your competitors could copy you.

That may still be true about some processes, like drug-development or a highly sophisticated manufacturing method, but X-engineering turns the rule about process secrecy on its head. The new rule: Be open about all your processes except those that are clearly proprietary. The reason for this openness is valid and irrefutable. In the X-engineered world, as Donnelley and others have discovered, you need to integrate your processes with those of your customers and suppliers, and sometimes even with the processes of your competitors. You need to know what they are doing and vice versa. This is simply not possible under the old rules of protect and defend. Also, most of your processes aren't unique, so there is no benefit to hiding them.

In times past, process was defined in terms of a single company's operations; now it describes the operations of a whole collection of companies, all constantly interacting with each other. There is a new trans-organizational flow-through to processes. No longer are they seen as discrete and stand-alone but rather as part of a continuum—interdependent and responsive to other processes.

In this sense, X-engineering echoes the principles of ecology.

Just as the whole edifice of nature consists of interdependent elements, so a company's collection of processes relies on other companies' collections of processes to survive. In fact, in many key processes, such as distribution, procurement, and new-product development, this symbiosis develops into something close to a union.

To make that notion tangible: Your business will thrive only if the processes used by the company that buys from you and the company that sells to you thrive. For your company to operate at peak efficiency and to maintain its competitive advantage, the processes of these inside-outsiders must also be efficient and aligned with yours. Using technology to improve this inter-organizational performance is a key element of X-engineering.

As I mentioned in Chapter 1 and will discuss later in this book, incredible inefficiencies exist between companies and their customers, suppliers, and partners. Many of these inefficiencies will not disappear until industries can agree on standardized processes—a challenge that goes well beyond that of traditional reengineering.

The challenge may alarm some managers, but it is certainly not insuperable. Companies within the same industry already perform many of the same processes, most of which provide no distinction or competitive advantage. Moreover, opportunities abound to create process-based ventures that avoid the replication of infrastructure. Banks realized this years ago when they established "clearinghouses" for financial transactions. But even in the financial-services industry, many more processes could be shared in so-called "back room" operations. In the brokerage business, for example, a stock trade is a stock trade; in the insurance business, a claim is a claim; in the residential mortgage business, an application is an application. Why does every brokerage, insurance company, and mortgage provider have to build its own processes? Billions and billions could be saved if companies collaborated and shared the processes that are now essentially redundant.

As you look more closely at processes, you will see many different types. It is important to know how they contribute to the performance of your business and how they interrelate to your suppliers' and customers' processes. Some are operational and deal with the movement of physical products, such as the process of order fulfillment. Others, like performance review, are managerial, dealing with information. Still other processes address customers directly, such as customer acquisition and service. Then there are those, including most processes in finance and human resources management, that are used to run a company. You can't manage a business without most of these processes, but some will be more important to your company than others.

To help you determine the relative importance of your many processes, I divide them into three basic groups:

- The processes you perform yourself. They may still be unique to your company, providing a competitive advantage. They are so important that you want to control them yourself and not trust others to do them.

- The processes you perform with others. They involve the transfer of information, goods, or money between your company and your suppliers, partners, and customers. These processes may be important to your company, but you may no longer want to consider them proprietary.

- The processes others perform for you. These processes may or may not be central to your operations, but they are not your core competency. Another company performs these processes better—and possibly less expensively—than you do. That's because these processes are its principal business. So you may choose to outsource these processes to that organization.

X-engineering calls for a reexamination of all three types of processes. Of those that you perform yourself, you must ask, Is this process really proprietary? Could it be performed more efficiently if it was opened up to suppliers or customers? Could it be shared with others? Of those that you perform with others, the questions should be, How far should I go in harmonizing these processes with customers, suppliers, or partners? Has the process been fully integrated into the electronic infrastructures of all the affected parties? Of those processes that others perform for you, you must ask: Is my supplier for this process capable of X-engineering it in partnership with me, my other suppliers, and customers?

These questions, together with others posed in this book, are crucial, and the answers to them will help you develop your X-engineering strategy. The key here is a top-to-bottom inventory and revaluation of all of your processes. In the end, you may not choose to redesign all of them, but it is important to know how they perform as a key to opportunity. (More on this topic in a later chapter.)

One company that has X-engineered its processes is Cessna Aircraft Co., a plane-making pioneer that is now a $2-billion-a-year subsidiary of Textron, Inc. In the late 1990s Cessna realized that its traditional, hierarchical management structure wasn't up to dealing with its 5,000-odd suppliers, whose costs and prices were rising even as quality was falling and only 45 percent of deliveries were arriving on time.

The traditional answer to rising prices would be to whipsaw suppliers through competitive bidding. But Cessna realized that approach would only result in corner-cutting, which would make the proportion of defective parts even worse than the current horrendous 5 percent that were arriving at the time. Suppliers could also find new ways to get back their reduced margins by such measures as billing separately for each subassembly or padding their own costs. David L. Oppenheim, Cessna's director of e-commerce, summed it up this way: "If a supplier is forced to reduce its price by eating its margin, costs are not reduced but only moved—and will bounce back again and again."

So Cessna set out on a five-year X-engineering project to transform not only its supply chain but its own corporate culture by integrating the suppliers into Cessna's entire design-and-manufacturing process. In effect, Cessna chose to share some of the proprietary processes it had formerly kept to itself and to cede more control over shared and outsourced processes. The suppliers were no longer regarded as mere producers of parts but as adders of value to the shared enterprise.

Within its own management Cessna set up cross-functional commodity teams for purchasing, managing sourcing and supply, and integrating and improving performance of the suppliers in each sector. Paperwork was pared and automated, partnering and long-term contracts replaced the bidding process, and a Six Sigma quality improvement program did away with redundant tests and inspections. An electronic data interchange (EDI) system, combined with Cessna's Web site, allowed all the suppliers to communicate with each other and ended all the business formerly done via phone or fax. Schedules were now shared electronically, and all the data was centralized in an executive information system open to the whole supply chain.

The suppliers met regularly to raise the performance bar on quality, productivity, and collaborative engineering, and this evolved into a system of shared decisions in Cessna's planning, designing, and manufacturing processes. All along the supply chain, partners were encouraged to work with each other to X-engineer their processes. Strategy was set in annual supplier conferences—at which, significantly, Cessna listened to its suppliers and adopted many of their suggestions.

At that point, Cessna was a new company. But midway through the five-year plan, Michael Katzorke, vice president for supply chain management, observed that Cessna's management system designed for the 1970s had changed only enough to meet the demands of the mid-90s. "The not-so-good news is, we have a long way to go," he added. "But our whole internal infrastructure is coming together, and in two years we'll be up there with the best of them. We must stay the course."

In truth, however, that will still be only a beginning. Just as in ecology, the change is unending; each new configuration of business processes inspires and requires another. X-engineering will never be finished.

Proposition

Let's look at the second corner of the X-engineering triangle, the juncture where you determine the business proposition that you offer your customer and the basis on which you can achieve breakthrough operational performance. Whatever your business proposition may be, it will stand or fall in the end on its ability to create new value for customers.

There are at least seven universal value propositions: customization, innovation, price, quality, service, speed, and variety. These propositions often determine how you are perceived by your customers, and they can define your basis of competition. Companies working together can achieve results that elude them when working alone as well as deliver additional value to customers.

Wal-Mart Stores, Inc., with its "always low prices" business proposition, is a case in point. Samuel Moore Walton didn't invent discount retailing, but he was obsessed with delivering more and more value to his customers—and since his death, his company has gone its founder one better. Using technology to facilitate interaction with its suppliers, the company continually streamlines its supply chain to drive operating and inventory costs lower and lower. It combines technology with redesigned procurement and distribution processes to achieve dramatic improvements in efficiency and support the low-cost mandate of its business proposition.

In addition to cost- and efficiency-based propositions, companies can X-engineer to deliver value with other basic propositions—such as customization, service, and variety. A company that becomes superb at any one of my seven universal business propositions—or at a proposition not yet imagined—can lift itself above the crowd.

CUSTOMIZATION

Consider customization. Bertelsmann AG, the media and publishing behemoth, is working toward the day when customers can create their own CDs online, mixing and matching their favorite music and artists and allowing the company to compete with Internet businesses such as Napster. "Personalization is absolutely key to Bertelsmann as a business," says Andrew D. Dorward, director of personalization for the company's Web site, bol.com, told a reporter not long ago. "My vision would be a . . . media network which is different for whoever signs into it."

In computer networking, Cisco Systems, Inc.'s MarketPlace allows corporate customers to create a precise combination of routers, switches, and hubs based on their needs. And as these needs evolve, MarketPlace is right there, ready to provide the upgrades, adjustments, tweaks, and any bells and whistles the customer desires.

As the Internet and X-engineering converge, there will be opportunities for customization that allow companies to approach the long-sought market of one—a unique product tailored for each customer.

SERVICE

Service as a business proposition should be all about getting to know your customers so well that you can solve their problems and satisfy their needs better than anyone else. And these benefits are by no means limited to high-tech companies. Alamo Rent-A-Car Company is a case in point. Much of that company's business comes through big tour operators who package the services of hotels, airlines, and car rental agencies. Formerly, this required Alamo and its competitors to set up elaborate back-office operations to handle endless paperwork, such as redeeming coupons and paying commissions.

For Alamo's tour-operator customers, this was an essential service. For Alamo, it was a grinding nuisance—a boring but necessary process that was usually done inefficiently, adding no value for the end-use customer, the vacationer actually driving an Alamo car, and very little value for the tour operators. Then Alamo's managers thought of a way to X-engineer this dead end into a creative process with a competitive advantage. They redesigned the back-office work to support a new business proposition to win over more tour operators.

In 1998 Alamo went online with E-Process 2000. It included a variety of services for tour operators, including electronic reservation links, voucherless rental processing, and electronic billing. The operators could dispense with paper vouchers—they were all archived on an Internet site. The packagers work on notoriously slim margins, and the new Alamo site made it possible for them to get paid instantaneously.

In other words, Alamo made it far simpler and faster for tour operators to order cars, cash in vouchers, and collect their money. The result was predictable: E-Process 2000 enormously increased Alamo's business with these groups.

VARIETY

Finally, consider variety. The Internet makes it possible for buyers to browse through a planet-size bazaar crammed with every imaginable product at every imaginable price. Surfing through cyberspace, they can buy anything from acorns to zithers without ever leaving their computers. But is this what buyers really want? Not quite. Yes, they want variety, the Internet's strength. No, they don't want bewildering variety, the Internet's weakness. In short, they love choice, but they want an efficient process for choosing.

Variety is an excellent business proposition—but only if a process is in place to assist the customer in narrowing the choices or making a selection that fits her own taste. There is ample recent evidence, in the form of the failure of many e-tailers, that customers who feel overwhelmed by shopping online simply abandon it. And winning back a customer is twice as difficult and expensive as attracting her in the first place. So filtering and vetting of choices becomes of paramount importance.

Major League baseball is a prime example of an industry that has X-engineered across a thicket of corporate boundaries to create a unified customer experience. Its Web site offers the league's full variety, but it is carefully controlled and filtered so that fans of all kinds can easily interact with it.

None of that was easy. For openers, the 30 independent teams get along uneasily at best. Struggling small-market teams covet the clout and revenues of teams in major cities. All of them fight bidding wars for the top talent, some are rivals for fans in a major geographic area, and in the past they have fought bitterly over how to divide any new revenues that come their way.

Baseball provides the ideal subject for a Web site. Its 73 million fans devour a host of comparative statistics, and the game provides literally millions of fresh facts to be logged during its seven-month season. In the past, however, the individual Web sites have been fragmented and have varied widely in quality, ranging from highly professional interactive meccas to mom-and-pop sites with limited appeal.

The breakthrough came in 2000, when MLB commissioner Bud Selig persuaded all 30 owners to agree to collaborate on a combined site, and even to share the revenues equally. Since estimates are that the site could be generating as much as $1 billion annually by 2006, that was a real milestone—what Selig calls "a very dramatic change in thinking."

And the site materialized in remarkably short order. When the 2001 season opened, fans clicking on their own team's name were sent to the team's page on the new, integrated site, which features a consistent look and feel for all the teams. The site provides statistics, interactive games, audio broadcasts, and video highlights. Some of it comes free, but other features are available only by subscription. A fan can focus on her own team or browse among its rivals, picking and choosing from a clear and orderly menu. The Web site www.mlb.com is a great example of providing variety without bewilderment and demonstrates that process standardization can be achieved even between real competitors.

Participation

As you consider all your processes and identify the proposition that you will offer your customers, you must also consider who will participate with you in X-engineering. How extensively do you plan to cross organizational boundaries? What partners do you want to involve in your business redesign and operations? I have identified four different levels of participation that I will dis-cuss and illustrate with examples in Chapter 8. Here's a preview: At Level 1 a company redesigns its own processes. At Level 2 it redesigns its processes along with the processes of another type of organization (say, a customer or a supplier). At Level 3 a company redesigns its processes along with the processes of two other types of organizations (suppliers and customers, for instance). At Level 4 a company redesigns its processes along with the processes of three other types of organizations (customers, suppliers, and partners). Needless to say, the more diverse the participants and the larger their number, the greater your challenge—but also the greater the opportunity.

At Level 4, for example, with so many potential participants, it becomes possible to change the processes of an entire industry. Traditional industries are often the best candidates for this degree of reinvention. The change is usually driven by a powerful indus-try player or by a new participant that, utilizing a strong informa-tion technology infrastructure, pulls in other industry players, sometimes making them partners, sometimes acquiring them.

A well-known example of a company at Level 4 is eBay, Inc. As recently as five years ago the auction business was a commercial backwater inhabited by art and auction houses at the high end and flea markets at the bottom. But in an amazingly brief span of time, eBay not only transformed and expanded the industry but also invented the online auction format and created the world's largest personal online trading community.

Essentially, eBay is simply an Internet forum where sellers can find people interested in buying their goods and reach a deal. eBay itself remains strictly a middleman, thus avoiding all the stresses of procurement, sales, inventory, order fulfillment, and shipping. Its modest fees on each transaction provide it a tidy profit.

Remaining above the fray of its own marketplace, eBay doesn't inspect the merchandise or vouch for either buyers or sellers. The closest it comes to evaluation is to permit feedback from each side about the other for future buyers and sellers to inspect. But by being first in its field and expanding rapidly, it has capitalized on a virtuous cycle: The growing volume of goods attracts more buyers, who bid up prices and attract more sellers, whose goods lure in more buyers, and so on indefinitely.

That process gives eBay a virtual lock on its market: No rival is likely to overtake it as long as the winning cycle keeps spinning. But that hasn't stopped a spate of imitators from offering auction-type offerings, including such established marketers as Amazon.com, Inc.; Dell Computer Corporation; Microsoft Corporation; J.C. Penney Corporation; and The Sharper Image, Inc. It is thanks to eBay, in fact, that so many people—buyers and sellers alike—even contemplate participating in auctions these days. It defines Level 4 of participation by changing the processes of the entire retail trade industry.

What Lies Ahead

Now that the Three Ps have properly triangulated your approach to X-engineering, let's briefly preview the journey ahead. Coming up:

CHAPTER 3:
X-ENGINEERING IN ACTION—SOLECTRON
Solectron, Inc., has X-engineered itself into a formidable power in the little-known electronic manufacturing services industry. Solectron is renowned for the efficiencies of its processes, which is no accident: More than any other company I know, Solectron focuses on processes—not only its own but those of its customers

and suppliers. Its seamless work across organizational boundaries offers lessons for managers everywhere.

CHAPTER 4:
THE PULL OF CUSTOMERS, THE PUSH OF PROCESSES

In an X-engineered business customers can call the shots without creating disruption and chaos. But this comes about only when managers understand the concept of customer pull and know how their company's processes must respond to it. All X-engineered businesses, however diverse, match the push of their processes to the pull of their customers, and Chapter4 illustrates that fact in cases ranging from automakers to financial-service companies.

CHAPTER 5:
THE ROUGH ROAD TO HARMONY

Just as conductors meld disparate musicians and instruments into a harmonic unity, X-engineers must get their processes to work together for operational consistency and integrity—in a word, harmony. Without it, efforts to work across boundaries may well spark more conflict than collaboration.

But creating harmony requires actions and attitudes that may make managers uncomfortable. You must start at home, getting your own house in order. Then comes openness, a willingness to make your processes transparent to others. Next you must accept standardization, both in process and technology. And finally you face a decision: how far to go in harmonizing your processes with others.

CHAPTER 6:
USING X-ENGINEERING TO CREATE VALUE

X-engineering efforts will be useless unless they produce value for your customers. In today's volatile economy, when your competitors never sleep, you can't stop creating new business propositions. But X-engineering gives you an edge, since it makes your company highly efficient and flexible, able to spot new customer pull and respond quickly. This chapter explains how you can create compelling propositions for your customers.

Chapter 7:
Where to Mark the *X*

You will find X-engineering's sweet spot when you can manage costs and create more value at the same time. This chapter shows where to mark the *X*—where X-engineering can deliver maximum savings and revenues.

Chapter 8:
How Many Boundaries Will You Cross?

Now that you know your company can't go it alone, what's next? Should you build, buy, or buddy? How should you choose partners, and how do good partners behave? This chapter includes case studies of companies that have answered these questions in different but effective ways, illustrating the great variety of paths to X-engineering.

Chapter 9:
What X-Engineering Demands from You

As a general rule, managers should use familiar business principles to deal with new circumstances, such as technological change. For one thing, the old principles have survived many alleged revolutions—as we saw in the late, unlamented dot-com bubble, when so many visionaries proclaimed the end of business as we know it and paid for their unwisdom.

Still, it would be folly to assume that a concept as disruptive as X-engineering would not call at least some management verities into question. And so it does: In fact, several well-known tenets must change dramatically if X-engineering is to succeed. This chapter explores the new mind-sets that managers need for X-engineering.

CHAPTER 10:
TEN MISTAKES EVERY X-ENGINEER SHOULD AVOID

Companies continue to stumble into the same pitfalls on the road to X-engineering. This chapter details the most common mistakes. Among the victims: companies that try to X-engineer before they reengineer; companies that create a separate e-business; and companies that move too slowly—or too quickly.

CHAPTER 11:
X-ENGINEERING IN ACTION—SCIQUEST

A few good Web-based companies have survived the dot-com bust. They are organized on sound business principles, are well run, and offer their customers a powerful value proposition. One model to emulate is SciQuest, Inc., a provider of scientific supplies, which has learned to make life easier for its customers by pulling together many partners for one-stop shopping in a highly fragmented marketplace.

CHAPTER 12:
X-ENGINEERING IN ACTION—
PNC FINANCIAL SERVICES GROUP

PNC Financial Services Group has transformed itself from a regional bank success to a multi-billion-dollar national powerhouse, mainly by mobilizing its people in a continuing campaign to X-engineer all its processes. Like most X-engineering stories, this one is just beginning—and if it ever ends, success will be finished, too. PNC knows that X-engineers must keep moving.

Now that you know where we are going, let's turn our attention to examples of how X-engineering has succeeded for a variety of companies in a variety of fields. You may not find that any of them exactly matches your own circumstances, but you will surely find ideas here that will help with your own campaign. What should encourage you is that these ideas are not all works of genius pioneered by brilliant companies that few others can hope to match.

In fact, this is one of the new business verities: As I study X-engineered businesses, over and over again I am struck by how technology has allowed once-ordinary companies to turn ideas into powerful new processes and propositions that quickly transform the companies themselves. In the next chapter, you can see this alchemy at work in the case of Solectron, which has X-engineered itself into a formidable manufacturing organization.

Chapter 3

X-Engineering in Action—Solectron

As the reengineering wave swept through the business world over the past decade, companies around the globe achieved quantum leaps in the quality and performance of their operations, and there was no way to to this without transforming their processes. As Lawrence A. Bossidy, the respected chairman of Honeywell, Inc., noted not long ago, "The competitive difference is not in deciding what to do, but in how to do it . . . Processes . . . are paramount."

There is no better case in point than Solectron Corporation, a quietly brilliant leader in the little-known field of electronics manufacturing services (EMS). Solectron and a handful of its competitors are the businesses that increasingly do the actual manufacturing of circuit boards, computers, routers, and communications infrastructure equipment sold under such familiar brand names as Cisco, Dell, and Nortel. EMS producers thrive by being faster, more efficient, and more flexible than their customers at turning out the customers' own designs and achieving the highest possible quality in the finished product. Solectron, in fact, is the first two-time winner of the coveted Malcolm Baldrige National Quality Award for manufacturing, and it is a company that views itself almost entirely in terms of its processes.

The EMS industry is, to some extent, a by-product of the focus on reengineering. When companies concentrate their efforts on the processes they do best and that are most crucial to their success, they are likely to farm out work that other companies can do just as well or better. In the electronics industry, the big original equipment manufacturers (OEMs) are concentrating on the design and sale of their high-tech wonders, increasingly leaving actual manufacturing to the EMS servicers. At last count, outside manufacturers were turning out about 10 percent of the $610 billion in hardware sold by the industry in 1998. But the EMS share was growing much faster than total electronic sales, so EMS should account for about half of the industry's production within 10 years.

In this chapter and at key points in those that follow I will use Solectron as an exemplar of the X-engineered corporation. To start with, let's examine Solectron's Three Ps, the areas of the company that make up its X-engineering triangle—process, proposition, and participation. Although I will consider each separately, in reality, the Three Ps never operate in isolation. They are dynamic and interwoven, supporting each other in the common cause. X-engineering separates them out to enable you to see them more clearly and thus manage them better.

Process

Solectron didn't originally set out to take in its neighbors' manufacturing. It was founded during the energy crisis of the late

1970s as a maker of solar energy products. But when the crisis eased and the solar market clouded up, Solectron's leaders decided to push into the booming electronics industry in nearby Silicon Valley. The company's first chief executive, Winston Chen, had learned both customer-centrism and a thorough under-standing of processes in his early career at the International Business Machines Corporation (IBM), and he instilled both creeds at Solectron.

You will recall that I defined processes as all the activities a company performs to create and sell its goods or services, and I have never seen a company more process-conscious than Solectron. Its people think of everything they do in those terms: Its processes have processes, and there are processes for initiating new processes. An outsider might be pardoned for suspecting that Solectron is too busy tending to processes to actually make anything—if it weren't for the fact that until the recent economic slowdown the company's revenues have grown consistently at a rate of more than 30 percent a year.

X-engineering divides processes into three basic categories:

1. the processes you perform yourself

2. those you perform with others

3. and those others perform for you

All three are on display at Solectron.

The main processes that Solectron keeps to itself relate to man-ufacturing—such esoteric, proprietary skills as making ball-grid arrays, chip-on-substrate, multi-chip modules, tape-automated bonding, and fine-pitch surface mount packages. These are indeed core competencies: Customers can safely assume that Solectron's manufacturing processes will be second to none.

And how did they get that way? In most cases, new processes come from new customers when they teach Solectron how to make their products. Once learned, the processes are then perfected with painstaking care, and, before long, Solectron can do the job faster and better than its customer can.

As new projects keep coming, a kind of cross-fertilization makes Solectron's people independent experts. In assembling printed circuit boards, for instance, early customers were always trying to reach new levels of technology, and Solectron would work with first one and then another to develop new processes, including such wonders as the automated assembly of printed circuit boards. (I will say more about this customer connection later in this chapter.)

The company's preoccupation with process finds its ultimate expression on the factory floor, where a work order is itself called a "process." It exists not on paper but in a computer, complete with the general information needed to carry it out, digitized diagrams and photographs, and a record of how the work was performed. And these days, the Solectron intranet features what is called the Process Web, with individual work orders linked into a hierarchy of related processes (for example, replenishment of inventories depleted on the job and invoices sent on completion). Thus anyone with access to the system can glean any information needed about any of Solectron's current projects. Design and engineering groups can get feedback from manufacturing, for example; action items can be traced and verified; multiple sites can use the same process and tap into the system from any plant in the network. And the Process Web is evolving into an informal bulletin board where news is posted, management communiqués are read, and workers trade anonymous tips and comments about their work.

Among the processes Solectron performs itself is the integration of an acquired factory into its operations. There have been literally dozens of occasions to use it: Customers ranging from

IBM and Nortel, Inc., to the Hewlett-Packard Company and Telefonaktiebolaget LM Ericsson have been so pleased with Solectron's outsource service that they have actually sold Solectron their plants. Solectron, in turn, uses the facilities to turn out goods for several customers rather than just one, achieving much higher efficiency and greater economies of scale than the original owner did.

But ownership transitions are never easy, as a spokesperson noted, and "we're very proud of how we handle them." Workers at the acquired facility usually feel demoralized and frightened of being laid off, while managers recoil from new standards and techniques and wonder whether adjusting will be worth the effort. A manufacturing director at what used to be NCR Corporation's plant in suburban Atlanta, Georgia, said he felt "kicked in the stomach" when NCR sold the facility to Solectron in 1997. But despair turned to enthusiasm when the director saw the enthusiasm that Koichi Nishimura, Solectron's chief executive, had for the plant and its possibilities. "It was a totally different perspective," the director remembered. "Rather than seeing us as a necessary evil—a cost center to be controlled—he saw us as a business in which manufacturing was the core competence."

Solectron's integration process begins with entrepreneurial doctrine: Plant managers are given the authority to run their operations almost as independent businesses. But first the plant's basic system is meshed with Solectron's infrastructure. As one Solectron manager explained: "The first thing we do is install phone systems, Internet connections, e-mail and voicemail, and so on. Then we bring in the business intelligence tools, our financial integration systems, the worldwide materials systems. We want end-to-end capability for integrating systems and processes within those companies." (Chapter 5 will address the importance of this move, the need to standardize technology platforms in order to make X-engineering work.)

Among the processes that Solectron performs with others, the most significant speak to its relationship with its customers. It all begins with Solectron's sales process, a courtship ritual as intricately programmed as an exotic bird's mating dance.

Sales representatives (called account managers) target customers, develop contacts, and offer presentations. "But the customers would never buy anything until they've actually touched and felt what they will get in terms of service," said Susan Wang, the chief financial officer. The sales process evolves very rapidly into an operational audit.

Teams from both companies study each other's operations and methods; the customer sends teams to Solectron factories to observe and ask questions without limit. If the customer moves on to propose a specific job, both sides study it and discuss how it should be done, and the plans go through as many design and revision loops as necessary before a price is quoted. "They ask us then to do a sample run, just to see how well it comes off our production line," said Wang. "In this process, every level of our management meets with every level of their management. So we have CEO-to-CEO meetings, CFO-to-CFO, engineering manager to engineering manager, production supervisor to production supervisor, all the way down to the foreman level."

This is all part of a multi-step Solectron process for customizing its production to a customer's needs. It includes careful analysis of basic compatibility with the customer, the needs of a particular job and the merits of the solutions proposed, a prototype assembly run, design refinement, personnel training, production controls, and—always—a built-in process for improving the original process. And any product new to Solectron triggers a separate new-product introduction process, with the company's own engineers participating with the customer's staff in designing the product, selecting materials and suppliers, and staying with the project through the early stages of production.

Only when everyone is completely comfortable does the actual production begin. During the production run, Solectron employees so completely assume responsibility for the job that they actually tell visitors that they work for the customer. And throughout the run, the customer's employees are welcome to roam the production line—asking questions, checking quality, making suggestions for improvement, or just watching.

Once a new customer is in the fold, it becomes the center of a customer focus team, which typically includes the Solectron people most concerned with that job—the project engineer, the program manager, the project buyer, workers from the production line, and representatives from manufacturing management, quality control, test engineering, production control, and sales.

This is no Potemkin committee. The customers themselves are partners in the process. Each customer fills out a weekly customer satisfaction index report, assigning grades (A through D) for quality, delivery, communication, service, and overall performance, with added comments as needed. The reports, communicated via Solectron's Web site, are formally reviewed with the customer at weekly meetings of each site's senior managers. Any score below a B gets immediate attention and prompts a quality-improvement process, and a score of C or lower triggers a formal customer complaint resolution process. The program manager is required to respond to the customer within 24 hours and must come up with a plan to resolve the complaint within 72 hours.

The weekly report cards are backed up by an even more formal annual customer survey, which goes to senior managers of each customer together with a letter from Solectron's chief executive, explaining the survey's importance and asking for cooperation. To ensure objective results, the survey is actually administered by an independent market-research firm, and the results are read like Gospel at Solectron headquarters.

Solectron is the ultimate outsource, the company that lives by

47

convincing other businesses to let it assume their manufacturing processes. But Solectron itself sometimes turns to outside organizations to perform processes that it believes they can do better and less expensively.

A prime example was the company's decision to hire IBM to create the information-technology infrastructure that connects customers and Solectron personnel around the world. It allows for master scheduling across multiple locations, materials planning, and the weekly customer report cards. It is available all day, every day, is impervious to hackers, and is contained within a structure safe from the effects of natural disasters such as earthquakes.

"We come from a site-centric background," Bernard "Bud" Mathaisel, Solectron's chief information officer, told me. "The people at our sites run their plants very well, but this new infrastructure called for specialized skills of a different magnitude. So we decided that this was something that another company could do better than we could, and we outsourced to IBM. You might say that we practice what we preach."

Proposition

The second corner of the X-engineering triangle represents the business propositions that you adopt to deliver new value for your customers. Chapter 2 listed seven key propositions that can be offered to customers. There are others, of course, but these are the most universal. They are: price, quality, service, customization, innovation, speed, and variety.

Now, let's look at examples of how Solectron has developed some of these business propositions and redesigned its processes to achieve both breakthrough efficiencies and industry-leading advantage as well as create new value for customers.

PRICE

EMS companies, which manufacture electronics products for brand-name customers such as Cisco Systems, Inc., Dell Computer Corporation, and IBM, are on a constant hunt for cost-saving opportunities. They start out, of course, with a substantial cost advantage over their customers. They gain economies of scale on materials and components because they handle projects for several OEMs and make better use of their manufacturing capacity. They also achieve better rates of capacity utilization. As a result, their total costs are 10 to 20 percent lower than what their customers normally spend to do the job themselves.

On the other hand, given the high level of competition, EMS companies have thin profit margins. Solectron, the leader, has an average margin of only 4 percent.

Raw materials represent a major chunk of the cost of the company's products, and Solectron is constantly seeking ways to adjust its systems to improve efficiency.

"Basically, MRP, and for that matter, ERP, is just execution to a set of specifications that are handed to it," said my friend Bud Mathaisel, the CIO. "You can tune the ERP all you want, and you might get 10 or 20 percent improvement if you can influence either the advanced planning model to do the what-if better or to do the component selection better."

Solectron is looking to double such savings by installing an information-technology system that links the company much more closely with its suppliers. The goal is to achieve real-time design collaboration, so that Solectron and its suppliers can mutually attack problems as they arrive and develop new ways to cut materials costs.

SPEED

Given their short life cycle, it is essential that electronic products be moved to market as quickly as possible. Estimates are that their market prices tend to shrink by about 1 percent a week. A circuit board that sits in a warehouse or the hold of a ship for a month can be underpriced by 4 percent by a newer equivalent; even worse, it may be well on the way to the fire sale of obsolescence.

So here again, materials are a crucial key. They represent the lion's share of Solectron's lead time with its customers. So the goal is to bring in raw material more quickly to assure sources of supply. Solectron's improved system is intended to help with that task.

Speed was a major consideration in Solectron's decision to build a network of more than 60 factories around the world. They make it possible for the company to respond rapidly to any of its customers' local marketing opportunities with the least possible movement of goods, by switching rapidly from one client's production run to the next job.

QUALITY

Since manufacturing is what they do best, EMS producers take pride in it. At its facilities in Milpitas, California, Solectron claims a phenomenally low defect rate of only 7 bad parts per million produced. By contrast, when *Industry Week* held a "best plant" competition in 1997, the median defect rate of the entries was 4,400 defective parts per million.

Solectron's commitment to quality has been essential to the company's success. And the Malcolm Baldrige National Quality Award, established by Congress to encourage the pursuit of excellence in U.S. business, has played a major role in helping the company make good on that commitment.

In 1989 Koichi Nishimura, the company's chief executive officer, and his managers applied for the Baldrige for the first time. He had no expectation of winning, he said later, but thought Solectron could make use of any criticism the Baldrige judges might offer, as a kind of free management consulting service.

Sure enough, the evaluators advised Solectron to pay more attention to its customers and to begin long-range planning for customer needs. Nishimura complied, and applied again next year. That brought more advice, which Nishimura followed again. He kept applying.

The Baldrige judges measure companies by seven criteria: leadership, strategic planning, customer and market focus, information and analysis, human-resource focus, process management, and business results. In 1991 the evaluators were sufficiently impressed by Solectron's entry to send an inspection team to visit the home plant. And after the team's report, Solectron became the first company in the electronics manufacturing services industry to win the prestigious award. In 1997 Solectron became the first repeat winner in the award's history.

The Baldrige awards have been an invaluable marketing tool for Solectron, but the company also uses them to ensure continuing quality improvement. Nishimura has adapted the Baldrige evaluation method as an internal process for recognizing excellence at Solectron.

Every two years, each site in Solectron's global system submits a formal application for the Solectron Total Quality Excellence Award (STQEA). The applications include full documentation of difficult jobs, innovation, customer satisfaction, and outside recognition of achievement. A board of examiners made up of 37 of Solectron's senior managers then assigns internal examiners to evaluate and score the applications, visit sites, and produce feedback reports, applying all seven of the Baldrige criteria.

The awards are cherished by the winners, but the process itself is the real prize. Since executives are both applicants and examiners, they learn from each other in the competition—and what the company learns figures largely in Solectron's long-range planning. In the national contest, Baldrige winners are not allowed to enter the competition again for five years, so Solectron won't be eligible until 2003. It is the STQEA, Nishimura has said, that keeps the company on its toes in the off years.

For Solectron, rooted in manufacturing, the three propositions above—price, speed, and quality—are key. Its ability to redesign its processes to make the most of these propositions has given the company lasting advantage in its industry.

That is not to say, however, that Solectron has failed to make the most of other business propositions. We have seen how it has created processes to offer customers an almost infinite variety of supply chain service approaches, while designing other processes that assure customers of immediate, complete service.

When company officials talk about innovation, for example, they point to plans to more closely link computer aided engineering systems with manufacturing systems and similar plans to improve links with customers. But the software itself, they insist, is not the real key to innovation; software is available to anyone in the industry. The magic comes in the thought and experiences Solectron brings to using the software.

"I can buy the same golf clubs as Tiger Woods," Bud Mathaisel told me, "but I can't play his game. Innovation is not in the tools—it's in the use of the tools."

Participation

The third corner of the X-engineering triangle concerns the outside organizations that you want to take part in your business. Thus Solectron has developed close links with its major outside participants, its customers and suppliers. It has created systems to gain extensive and precise information on their financial condition, materials needs, and order books, learning to interface with their diverse systems to keep the chain working smoothly.

Solectron's supply base management process, for example,

uses teams organized around key commodities, and its aim is to progress from short-term transactions with suppliers to long-term relationships built on open communication, trust, overall capability, and total cost of ownership.

At the same time, Solectron is giving customers access to key data on its Web site, including the production status of orders, pricing information, and quality updates.

The company is also participating in RosettaNet, a Web-based network of electronics companies that is developing common processes for aligning supply chain partnerships. "We're talking about business processes that go beyond purchase orders, things such as collaborative planning and shared inventory management," one Solectron manager explained.

RosettaNet provides a common language for reaching across technological barriers. This means that companies are not limited to dealing with suppliers whose systems they can reach; they can talk to anyone on the network and choose suppliers on the basis of customer service. And given all the information now available, business relationships have the potential to reach a whole new plane: "You understand your customers' requirements and needs in such a way," that same manager said, "that you can provide a service they may never even have imagined."

In this chapter, I have suggested some of the ways in which Solectron constantly X-engineers itself. As you have seen, the company has pursued that goal on every level of the X-engineering triangle, from process to proposition to participation. Yet, I have only just begun to describe the ways in which companies are moving to meet the challenges of today's volatile economic environment. You will hear more about Solectron and other remarkable organizations in the chapters ahead.

Chapter 4

The Pull of Customers, the Push of Processes

From the time the first business opened its doors all those centuries ago, people have been trying to define the essence of a company. Some have claimed that a business is its bottom line. Others have argued that a company is its customers, or its marketing power, or its products, or its people.

Today what best defines a business is its processes—all the things a company does to create and sell its goods and services. And X-engineering is focused directly on those processes.

In the course of viewing and participating in X-engineering projects at a number of corporations, I have observed that very different processes, such as order fulfillment and new-product development, have been changed in strikingly similar ways. That has held true for all kinds of X-engineered processes in all kinds of industries, for the auto manufacturer as for the financial-services company or retailer. In other words, X-engineered processes have much in common. Specifically, they share two crucial characteristics:

- They are pulled by the customer.

- They push across organizational boundaries.

In this chapter, I will explore and explain both of these essential traits and provide case histories to illustrate how they manifest themselves in the corporate setting.

The notion that companies should be "customer driven" has been heavily promoted, but ranks near the top on any list of most-ignored management dicta. As recently as 50 years ago, customers were seldom in the picture when new products were designed. Managers working for suppliers and manufacturers dictated when goods would be produced, how much they were going to cost, and what features they would offer. The marketing and salespeople were seldom consulted until after the fact.

In plain terms, manufacturers were pushing goods toward the customers—an arrangement that had certain advantages for the pushers. Among them, it simplified matters. The nature of their production processes and facilities determined how much of which product they would turn out. On the other hand, as a way to do business pushing had some serious shortcomings. For one, it often created a glut of inventory, which required warehouses to hold the goods until someone bought them. That was expensive. The producer-push approach also created a deep ocean of customer discontent.

In the 1960s all that began to change. Manufacturers started thinking in terms of consumer demand, including what they knew about their customers' tastes in the product design equation. In my reengineering days I added my voice to those who urged managers to become more customer-centered. I used to encourage managers to do "right-to-left" thinking—anything to convince them to consider processes from the outside in, from their customers' perspective.

Over the last decade that old cliché "the customer comes first" has actually come to pass. Producer push has come to customer pull: Products get manufactured because customers want them, not the other way around. Manufacturers go to great lengths to find out just what customers want, and then they tailor their goods to match.

Explaining that change, James P. Kelly, chairman and chief executive officer of United Parcel Service, Inc., compares today's global economy to a giant conveyor belt carrying products, services, and information. "It is a conveyor belt in constant motion," he said, "and it connects upstream and downstream business partners who perform specialized processes in a common enterprise." What's more, he said, "It's a conveyor belt moving in the direction—and at the control—of the end customer."

The arrival of e-commerce has only underscored the customer's new power. Now, electronically connected to the markets, both consumers and business customers use this access to shop actively for the features they want, the best price, and the vendor that will provide them. It is customer pull incarnate, with customers pulling on processes to gain the value that they want.

That might seem good for customers and bad for suppliers and manufacturers, but, in truth, it benefits all parties. To stay in business, suppliers have no choice but to tighten up, root out inefficiencies, and begin to cooperate, and that turns out to be good for the bottom line. Inventories are trimmed, costs cut, and time-to-market reduced.

In a vivid image, Kelly has said that when UPS first understood that the customer was now in charge, it was like driving down a superhighway and suddenly seeing the traffic coming right at you. "Rather than crash, we decided to turn around," he said dryly. And that meant that suppliers would have to rely on information and information technology: "They have to forge intimate electronic connections with each other, using shared information systems to orchestrate the flow of the production cycle."

In other words, they must respond to customer pull and develop cross-organizational process push.

X-engineering requires would-be partners to change many if not most of their processes; the relative importance of the three categories of processes described in Chapter 2 has to shift. Each partner company will probably find that it has fewer proprietary processes—those that are unique to it and essential to its competitive advantage—but the proprietary processes it retains will be fiercely defended. It will probably discover that many of its processes can be performed better and less expensively by other companies, allowing the company to concentrate on what it does best and uniquely. And, finally, the shared processes used by all of the linked businesses, from the customer to the manufacturer's suppliers, will have to be standardized so that they will mesh smoothly and effectively.

The Pull of Customers, the Push of Process at EMC

Once this change is complete, the X-engineered company ends up with processes that operate according to customer pull and that push across corporate boundaries to connect with suppliers, partners, and customers.

Now, let's see how those two common aspects of X-engineering play out in a real company setting—at EMC Corporation, the leading producer of computer memory storage devices. Based in Hopkinton, Massachusetts, EMC has a 30 percent share of a market that is expected to mushroom to $100 billion a year by 2005.

The company's founders, Richard Egan and Roger Marino, were roommates at Boston's Northeastern University. They have kept unblinkingly focused on a fact that most of the information-technology industry has tended to ignore: What the customers really want is information, and technology is merely the way to get it. Using that insight, and keeping constant watch on developments that can give them a momentary advantage, the two have reinvented their company and its processes every two years. As a result, they have managed to stay well ahead of such formidable competitors as International Business Machines Corporation (IBM), the Hewlett-Packard Company, and Sun Microsystems, Inc.

In the early 1980s the fledgling EMC (there's no third partner; the initials are for Egan Marino Company) saw its first big opportunity. The major computer makers, mesmerized by their own technological prowess, were gung-ho for the glamorous business of ever faster and ever more powerful number crunching, but they shrugged off information storage and retrieval as a boring sideline. They knew that all those 1s and 0s were useless unless they were kept somewhere, but memory made no headlines in those days, and customers were too busy trying to grasp the new field of information technology to pay much heed to storage.

Egan and Marino saw a chance to break into the business by commoditizing what the majors thought of as proprietary technology. Prime Computer, Inc., for instance, then a leading-edge computer maker, was selling add-on memory for the whopping price of $36,000 per megabyte. The academic researchers who used Prime computers couldn't afford that, and when one of them complained about it to Egan, the lightbulb lit up; it was the first but far from the last example of EMC's reaction to customer pull. The two partners toiled for five months to develop their own technology for a memory-storage device that would be compatible with the Prime system.

What they came up with had four times the capacity of Prime's memory unit at half the cost. After fending off a lawsuit from Prime, EMC was on its way.

The next major step was the then-neglected field of disk storage, which Egan and Marino saw as their way into the corporate market where the big money was. And that involved a frontal assault on giant IBM, which the partners saw as vulnerable because of its growing haughtiness and indifference to its customers. IBM fought back ferociously, with price cuts and rapid product improvements, but, in the end, EMC pushed its process to turn out a new disk storage system compatible with IBM. The corporate customers began arriving, responding to EMC's process push.

As the customers kept clamoring for more storage capacity, EMC stole a march on the whole field with a revolutionary idea. Having sensed the limits of disk size during its development of the IBM-compatible drive, EMC's technicians gave up that race and instead linked a number of smaller disks together in what is called RAID, a redundant array of independent disks. It was fast, reliable, and low-cost, and it was all theirs—a breakthrough in accessing, transferring, and storing large quantities of mainframe computer data. By 1994 EMC had erased IBM's lead in mainframe storage.

But EMC also knew that in high technology, any proprietary advantage is almost surely fleeting. It will inevitably be copied or outmoded in a matter of months. The only way to keep the lead is to stay so closely attuned to your customers that you become part of their business, part of a common enterprise that fills the needs of the end customer. And one of the ways to achieve that goal, as we shall see, is to push your processes across company boundaries to engage with the processes of your customers.

EMC's executive chairman Mike Ruettgers—he served as chief executive officer from 1992 to 2001—meets personally with 500 customers each year to make sure EMC understands their concerns and responds to their needs. One way the company seeks to stay ahead of its market is to sponsor academic research in the data-storage field. More to the point, it has set up "customer advisory councils" that are an impressive exercise in customer pull. They are unique in their combination of mutual trust, shared data, and common enterprise.

The councils are themselves shared processes. Twice a year, the company invites the visionaries and decision makers from 50 to 60 of its client companies to join EMC's top people for 20 hours of intense discussion spread over two and a half days. These are no picnics: The executives sign confidentiality agreements, and instead of tennis racquets and golf clubs they bring their assigned and completed homework projects. They talk about the industry's specific problems and whether EMC is doing enough to address them, and the discussion includes details of its work in progress. EMC probes the impact that its solutions might have on its customers and whether the clients have any partners who should also be brought into the process. And all of that information becomes part of EMC's strategic planning.

It was that kind of attention to the customers that led EMC to its next big insight, in the early 1990s, when personal computers were popping up on corporate desks and largely displacing central mainframes. The advantages of this were obvious, but EMC heard its customers complaining that there was also a downside: PCs were creating isolated pools of storage, with growing amounts of data inaccessible to the company at large. What companies needed was centralized data, accessible to everyone instantly at all times of the day.

EMC set out to develop "enterprise-wide" storage systems. Well ahead of the pack, it perceived that these also had to be standardized—that the centralized storage would have to be compatible with all sorts of hardware and software, so that all kinds of systems could feed into it. Various divisions could then follow their own computing tastes, new acquisitions could fit seamlessly into the system, and, as the Internet grew in importance, data could be communicated across corporate boundaries to clients, suppliers, and partners using multiple information-technology systems for shared processes, all feeding to and from a centralized repository of information.

That vision led to EMC's development of its own software and to its storage systems, near-miraculous boxes that are actually independently intelligent corporate memories. Each box, about the size of a refrigerator, can hold up to 69.5 terabytes—69.5 trillion bytes—of data, more than three times as much information as is contained in the entire Library of Congress. (Ruettgers likes to point out that in the infancy of the computer 40 years ago, it would have taken a device the size of Argentina to store just one terabyte.)

Symbolizing EMC's solicitude for its customers as well as the cross-organization push of its processes, each of these boxes has an "E.T., call home" feature: If something is going wrong in its innards, it literally telephones an EMC service center and alerts the technicians there. They will either fix the problem by remote control or make a house call, free of charge—which is probably the customer's first inkling that his or her storage system was about to crash. As EMC sees it, its customers have better things to do than worry about their computer systems.

Large customers with hugely complex electronic systems pose a special challenge, since any change in such a network is apt to have unforeseen and possibly damaging ripple effects. Dealing with that challenge requires cross-corporate cooperation, even among competitors. Whenever possible, EMC collaborates with the major hardware and software companies to build and install complete infrastructures, making sure all the parts work together. But that is often impractical; information technology is such a major factor in big companies today that it can rarely be ripped out and replaced at one stroke. If a customer's IT infrastructure must be altered, EMC technicians offer to preview the change and test any planned features in their own labs, setting up an IT infrastructure that matches the customer's for the test. With more than one billion dollars invested in its testing and qualification labs, EMC guarantees the customer a smooth migration to any technology that is connected to EMC's storage systems.

As EMC sees it, the future will bring more of the same—namely, constant change. The cost of a megabyte of storage, which as I write has been cut from that mammoth $36,000 to 40 cents, should be down to a single penny by 2005. Ruettgers visualizes demand for vast storage warehouses linked to the Internet and used by multiple companies. He sees each big company's information-technology system evolving into "e-infostructure," a web of high-tech tools and information that becomes a kind of corporate nervous system, pervading and enabling every decision and action taken. Before long, he predicts, the hum of the "universal data tone" will be heard in every corporate room and corridor as pervasively as the telephone dial tone is heard today.

Ruettgers also knows that the world can lurch off in sudden, unexpected directions. So EMC is placing bets on several major possibilities and tuning its processes to be ready to change accordingly. What remains constant in EMC's strategy? Simply this: producing high-quality products at competitive prices and creating distinctiveness through process.

Customer pull and cross-corporate push make EMC's X-engineered processes look vastly different from traditional business processes. Besides producing the extreme efficiency that competitive pricing requires, X-engineered processes at EMC and other organizations:

- represent the active collaboration of all the parties they engage and affect

- foster lower costs and greater customer value

- improve the business performance of all members of a supply chain

- rely substantially on information technology

- often call upon customers and/or employees to adopt a self-service mode

- provide feedback about performance and quality

You will find these characteristics illustrated in the examples throughout this book.

The Pull of Customers, the Push of Processes at Dell Computer

We have seen how X-engineering has played out at EMC. Now let's take a fresh look at a more familiar pioneer, Dell Computer Corporation, through the lens of X-engineering—and show how Michael S. Dell allows his customers to pull the company's processes and how he, in turn, pushes Dell's processes across multiple organizations.

When Michael Dell talks about his company, he has a favorite sentence that describes its relationship with the businesses that buy most of Dell's products and those that make the components for those products. "The Internet," he often says, "has allowed us to bring our customers and our suppliers inside our business to achieve shared efficiencies and greater loyalty." His organization was practicing X-engineering long before I coined the term. In fact, Michael Dell may be the original X-engineer. He launched his company on a customization (build-to-order) business proposition, and he developed the processes that were key to delivering that proposition well ahead of his competitors. Now, he is going further.

For example, in the customer realm, Dell is setting the pace with Premier Pages on its Web site, one for each major customer. (Michael Dell explains: "They're not going to go to a public Web site and order 50,000 PCs.") On these pages, of which there are now more than 100,000, customers can look over product choices configured to their particular needs, put through automated purchase orders, track the status of their orders, review the number and location of Dell machines in place in their operations around the world, and access and use service tools tailored for their Dell products.

The Premier Pages began as a support tool, allowing a Dell service person to call up a full history of the company's dealings with the customer—including purchase patterns and special requirements. The next step was to enable the customer to tap into Dell's troubleshooting and expert diagnostic tools via the Internet. The tools were then revised to use natural-language search engines. That was followed by the creation of online forums where Dell customers could talk over technical issues amongst themselves. The latest such online forum links up the experts who manage corporate helpdesks.

Today, Dell offers customers Premier Commerce pages, which make use of the data previously exchanged with each customer on its Premier page. The new pages are fitted up to offer goods that more precisely match the configurations required by the customer and to accommodate any complicated approval procedures. Beyond that, Dell has launched gigabuys.com, a site where customers can go shopping for products made by other companies that are compatible with Dell's machines.

In each case, the elaboration was intended to permit customers to initiate a connection with Dell when it was convenient for them and to make the decision as to how to seek assistance or obtain information or order product. "We've turned traditional manufacturing on its head," Michael Dell boasts. "We don't build anything until we get an order from a customer. We have a pull system as opposed to a push system."

The customer benefits of Dell's X-engineered processes are considerable, and not just in terms of convenience. Customers drastically reduce their expenditure of time and money. Orders that once took 21 days to submit can now be taken care of in less than two days. At the same time, Dell's own expenses have been slashed—an order status report that used to cost as much as $13 per telephone call, for example, now costs nothing—and that has helped Dell hold its prices down.

Dell has achieved even greater savings with its Internet-enabled connections with its suppliers, a prime instance of X-engineered processes pushing across and beyond a corporation's borders. As a result, the company was able to maintain its profitability in 2001 even as it ignited a price war by cutting personal-computer prices. Some 90 percent of Dell's suppliers are now Web-connected with the company's production lines. The result: Dell's inventories have plummeted from 13 days' supply in 1997 to 5 days' supply today, for a savings of $50 million a year.

The immense increase in the speed with which information is exchanged between Dell and its suppliers has greatly improved the efficiency of both parties. When there is a customer complaint about quality, for example, it rockets back through Dell to the appropriate supplier, who can then apply not just a quick fix but a total fix. By the same token, because suppliers learn of orders at the same time Dell does, they can instantly adjust their product mix to match the order flow, and Dell can maintain a minimal inventory.

The intimate link-up with Dell represents a great boon for suppliers as well, enabling them to better predict their requirements from their own vendors, which translates into smaller inventories. For suppliers—and for Dell and its customers—the Internet link has drastically cut costs.

The traditional relationship between manufacturer and supplier has not always been so cozy. Traditionally, manufacturers have been more concerned about price points than about supplier loyalty, and suppliers have shopped their expertise to the highest bidder. Even before the Internet came of age, Dell had gone a different route, giving suppliers a long-term order commitment in return for their commitment to quality of product, technological improvement, and reliable delivery. As part of the deal, Dell maintained a supplier certification program requiring that suppliers undergo occasional evaluations to make sure their operations met Dell's high standards.

Enter the Internet, and now the supplier evaluations are not occasional but continuous. Suppliers get their feedback in real time as Dell provides a constantly changing report card on their components' performance by region and line of business. Customers' comments also get passed along immediately. The incentive to meet Dell's standards is reinforced negatively as well as positively: Any less-than-perfect components go right back to the supplier. Michael Dell is clear about the company's relationship with suppliers. "They will last," he says, "as long as they maintain their leadership in technology and quality."

To do for its suppliers what Premier Pages do for customers, Dell has a Web site, valuechain.dell.com, on which suppliers can track Dell's orders and production plans and adjust their own operations to suit. More than 90 percent of Dell's raw materials come through suppliers using the site, which produced savings of $150 million by 2000—three years ahead of Dell's expectations.

Dell's process-push linkage with suppliers has paid other big dividends. In one 15-month period the company achieved a 40 percent increase in component quality. And the sharing of design ideas and production technologies has substantially reduced time-to-market. Still not satisfied, Dell is moving to apply similar standards to the vendors who serve its suppliers, further leveraging its connectivity to gain greater system reliability.

And all of this is still the early stages of Michael Dell's vision of X-engineering. In the long run, he and some of his colleagues foresee what they call friction-less trade—business so perfectly tuned by the Web that each company in a supply chain reacts automatically to incoming data, adjusts its operations, and speeds product to customers, all with hardly any human intervention.

This manufacturing nirvana is foreshadowed in Dell's state-of-the-art OptiPlex plant in Round Rock, Texas, an awesomely automated factory that churns out 20,000 computers on a typical day. Guided by electronic orders from 100 server computers, teams of workers assemble, customize, package, and ship the machines. The plant is the size of 23 football fields, but its command center is run by a mere half-dozen people. Most of the guidance comes from computers at Dell, its suppliers, and its customers. Automated, X-engineered processes handle orders, assemble parts from suppliers, organize production, and arrange packing and shipping. The plant operates with an inventory of two hours' worth of parts, held in a "warehouse" the size of a small bedroom, yet it can get out an order of hundreds of computers in as little as six hours.

The stock market turmoil and personal-computer sales slump of 2001 hit Dell along with its competition, forcing layoffs and reduced sales and earnings targets. But this has only intensified the company's efforts to boost efficiency. "To stay ahead, we have to keep running," Michael Dell said not long ago. He reacted to the looming crisis by actually starting a price war, counting on his corporation's efficiency to make a profit even as his rivals' margins turned to losses. Thanks to the OptiPlex plant, the strategy could work: The plant outproduces Dell's previous champion facility by fully 160 percent, per worker and per hour. Now, that's pushing processes.

All Companies Are Created Equal

It is a fair reaction, having read about the exploits of Dell, EMC, and Solectron, to say that your organization is different—that you aren't a high-technology company. So what does all this have to do with you? In truth, however, X-engineering applies at least as much to traditional industries, whose inefficiencies, and therefore opportunities, may be even greater.

There is no better example than the automobile industry. Its fossilized, rust-belt image is rapidly shredding as the big companies respond to customer pull and X-engineer their processes across corporate boundaries.

It has become conventional wisdom among automakers that the old way of doing business—pushing cars at consumers by producing whatever models they like and shipping them to dealers, no matter what their customers want—is obsolete. The new objective is building cars to order, and the producers' dream is to let each customer go online to order up an individual car, feature by feature, and take the wheel five days later.

That isn't going to happen any time soon, of course. The logistics are simply too formidable. At the Ford Motor Company, for instance, a joint project with United Parcel Service, Inc., aims to cut just the delivery time from factory to dealer down to eight days from a recent 15. But amazing progress toward building to order is being made.

Mitsubishi Motor Sales of America, a subsidiary of Tokyo-based Mitsubishi Motors Corporation, for instance, decided back in 1999 that producer push had to give way to customer pull. At that point, the stockpile of unsold cars on the docks and at Mitsubishi's plant in Normal, Illinois, and four other port cities had reached a total of 46,000. The dealer discounts needed to move them were decimating profit margins. Mitsubishi decided, said executive vice president and general manager Greg O'Neill, "We maybe weren't getting it right."

So Mitsubishi set up a new system that is at least partway along the road to building to customer orders. This allows the dealers to respond to their local markets, putting in orders for the cars they think will sell instead of having to peddle whatever the factory sends them. The lead time for orders is only five weeks, giving dealers flexibility to turn with the markets. And the dealers are happy. "It's wonderful," Marc Dubowy, who owns two dealerships in the Phoenix, Arizona, area, told a reporter. "We're getting the right cars that fit our market."

General Motors Corporation has moved even closer to building to order in its Brazilian operation. Its $600-million Blue Macaw plant, in the southern state of Rio Grande do Sul, is a pilot project for the company, building at least some low-cost Celta hatchbacks to customer orders in as little as three days.

Several factors make this easier in Brazil than it would be in the U.S. market. For one, the simple car offers few options and variations; for another, only 20 percent of the country's potential car buyers are wired to the Web and capable of online orders, a guarantee that the system won't be swamped. But GM's planners and engineers are studying the project and learning from it, and they hope to apply its lessons on a wider scale in future years.

Responding to customer pull promises enormous efficiency gains for the automakers. Ford alone will save $1 billion a year in inventory just by cutting the delivery time to dealers in half, and the industry estimate is that building to customer order could save an average $2,400 per car.

At least that much again could be saved if the industry could push its processes to optimize the supply chain that runs from raw materials through production plants to dealers and customers. By one estimate, the industry has a total of $700 billion in inventory in the supply chain at any given time—a hugely costly burden that some executives think could be cut by a third with existing technology.

In a move in that direction, GM, Ford, and DaimlerChrysler AG formed a much-publicized venture called Covisint. Initially a site for suppliers to auction their services, Covisint eventually will grow to be capable of full supply chain optimization. Other industry processes are also being transformed. The major companies are experimenting with direct online sales to customers, and GM has set up TradeXchange, an online site for auctioning vehicles coming off long-term leases. The corporation says it has saved $1,400 per car in the cost of transporting them to conventional auction locations. All told, the industry has made huge strides along the road to X-engineering, with much opportunity ahead

Now that you have a better sense of the two chief characteristics of an X-engineered organization—its reliance on customer pull and its process push across corporate boundaries—you will need to consider how to achieve an effective balance between pull and push. The next chapter will discuss some of the design approaches to follow. As you will see, balance translates to harmony.

Chapter 5

The Rough Road to Harmony

Managers may shy away from the word *harmony*. It has a certain softness that seems to defy the common perception that managing people and companies requires, above all, toughness—a greater concern for results than for feelings. But I'm talking here as much about the hard stuff—process—as I am about how you, your customers, and your partners feel about each other

The dictionary in my laptop devotes most of its definition of *harmonize* to a discussion of melodies and musical terminology. But it also includes the following: "to make rules, regulations, or systems similar or in accord with each other." That captures my meaning quite well, though, of course, I would add processes to the list.

As the first step in X-engineering, you must get your own processes to harmonize. You can't eliminate fragmentation, handoffs, and redundant work unless the processes within your organization work harmoniously together.

Once your internal processes are in harmony, it is time to move on to those processes through which you deal with outside organizations and individuals. That is, X-engineering calls for the harmonizing of your processes with those of your customers, partners, and suppliers.

Remember the lyric to Ira Gershwin's "Let's Call the Whole Thing Off"? "You say tomato, I say to-mah-to." Companies, like people, do and say the same things differently. Problems of service breakdowns and customer disappointments often occur because the processes involved just don't match up from one organization to another.

And why should they? To begin with, they were developed independently of each other. Beyond that, they represent polar opposite functions depending on which end of the process you occupy. After all, your sales processes are your customer's procurement processes. Your materials-inventory processes are your supplier's distribution processes. Your billing and receivable processes are your customer's payables processes. And your hiring processes are your prospective employees' job-search processes.

In order to harmonize, what is required is that these cross-business processes be harmonized, that they be redesigned to work in accord with each other. In some instances, that will mean making sure that your processes and the processes of your customers and partners connect well together when they interface or engage. For example, if your customers buy products in a certain manner and at certain times, your selling processes should be designed to fit those buying patterns. Recognize, however, that redesigning processes only at the interface may smooth out some rough spots between your operations and may produce some efficiencies, but it is highly likely that both your processes and the processes of your customers and partners were extremely inefficient to begin with.

For example, medical-supply companies have often found that

hospitals don't do a good job of ordering products. They may order small shipments too frequently and keep an oversupply of some products but run out of others. Driven by the personal preferences of thousands of physicians, they also can order too many different products. All of this increases the costs of procurement for both buyers and sellers and can drive down service levels. What's required in these instances is to step back and carefully examine all of the tasks both at the interface with customers (e.g., procurement) and related processes within your operation (e.g., inventory management). The aim is for both partners in each transaction to redesign and jointly own a new process (let's call it product management) that will cut costs and improve service. In Chapter 7 you will see this strategy in action at Owens & Minor, Inc.

In this chapter the focus is on how you can go about harmonizing your own processes and those you share with other organizations and individuals. I will also offer some examples of companies that have successfully done that. First, though, here are some of the actions you need to take to harmonize.

Apply Technology Intelligently

The application of technology to processes is an old story. In many instances it has proven its capacity for reducing cycle time and costs while improving quality. In other cases, it has made some processes so impenetrable that you need a pilot's course in navigation to find your way.

I am thinking of those automated processes that bounce you from one location to another, remnants of the departmentalization and fragmentation of work that still haunt so many companies. When I call my credit-card company to ask a complicated question, I inevitably get the bounce-around treatment and never do get to talk to a real person even if I need that level of service.

This kind of customer experience generally happens when a company applies technology to improve only its own efficiency and ignores improving its customer's efficiency—a poor example of harmonization.

X-engineering is not about automating old processes. Applying technology to old processes will result in an incremental efficiency improvement at best. X-engineering is about creating new processes that leverage information technology.

One advantage of technology-enabled processes is the capacity for self-service. Customers usually do know best what they need, and the more they do for themselves, the lower the cost should be to the supplier—and to them.

Technology also makes it much easier for a company to keep tabs on what its customers are buying. By organizing and analyzing that data, as well as through direct communications from customers, companies can learn a great deal about the kinds of products customers want—and about the kinds they don't want.

By using technology to harmonize supplier and customer processes, then, companies are responding to customer pull. They are able to use what they learn in interactions with customers both to respond to immediate needs and to determine what future markets will require. The information guides new product designs. In fact, in their responses to technology-enhanced processes, customers are also—automatically—taking a more active role in defining how these processes should work.

For most customers at Cisco Systems for example, Internet technology has become a way of life. Online sales account for 85 percent of Cisco's revenues.

That has happened, in part, because Cisco has so ingeniously melded its sales processes with its customers' procurement processes. In times past, software purchases were sent to customers on CDs by Federal Express. Now, software is downloadable from the software library on Cisco Connection Online

(CCO). Customers who formerly had to call customer service to follow up on hardware deliveries can now click on the Web site's Status Agent feature to check the status of an order and find a FedEx tracking number.

How far has Cisco taken the harmonization of its technology links with customers? It is actually hard for customers to make purchasing mistakes. If they select two or more items that don't work together, they are automatically warned. If they choose software that isn't compatible with the hardware their company previously purchased, they will receive an instant alert.

Indeed, it is one of the hallmarks of X-engineered processes that they anticipate possible customer problems and have appropriate responses ready and waiting. They foresee both the customer's needs and the customer's problems. The process harmony wrought by technology makes that possible.

Here are some questions to ask that may help you apply technology more intelligently.

- Am I using information technology to enable the design of new processes and to harmonize my processes with others, or am I just automating old processes?

- Am I investing in information technology before considering how processes must change in order to get the benefit out of my investment?

- Am I using information technology to allow customers, suppliers, and employees to do work for which they are better suited—a.k.a. self-service?

- Am I using information technology to gain real knowledge of the wants, needs, and expectations of my customers and suppliers?

Standardize Processes

Connectivity is the hallmark of X-engineered processes, and it is essential across the whole supply chain, from supplier to manufacturer to end user. A certain level of standardization is required to achieve the level of connection necessary for a smooth, full flow of information, product, and money. To make sure their customers and partners will know what to expect when they work together, companies will have to standardize processes. They will also have to standardize technology so they can communicate.

The technology part isn't so simple. Just think about XML, the language protocol that was to make it so easy for everyone to talk to everyone else on the Internet. It turns out that there have come to be so many individual versions of XML that it cannot truly be considered a standard for Internet communication. Unfortunately, this is true of many software and hardware products. Most large companies, particularly multi-divisional companies, have developed information infrastructures—software, hardware, networks, protocols—in a haphazard way. The result is multiple technologies, and even multiple versions of the same technology. Communicating *within* such companies is difficult, never mind communicating with other organizations. If yours is one of these companies, it will be necessary to standardize an internal technology platform before you try to harmonize your processes with others.

There is an even greater challenge in standardizing processes for all the companies involved in a supply chain, with all their different systems, different priorities, and different cultures.

The first factor to overcome is often psychological. In many companies, campaigning for "standardization" is about as popular and effective as shouting "Quiet!" at a rock concert. That is because there is a general perception that standardization crushes personal initiative and stifles creativity.

I recently saw that reaction at a large high-tech company that prides itself on its elevated level of innovation. Under that banner, every business function and every division pretty much did what it wanted in terms of developing and maintaining its own processes, systems, and technologies.

The company's product pipeline was full, but the organization was starting to have trouble simply doing business. Financial information, people, materials, and ideas moved with great difficulty and redundancy through the company—and the connections with customers and suppliers were even more cumbersome. There were constant arguments over the real meaning of the company's financial numbers, the true measure of customer satisfaction, and the best means of assessing employee performance.

The suggestion that processes be standardized touched off an uproar. Staff and employees assumed that process standardization would lead to greater centralization and control within the organization. Only later did they understand that standardization can be a liberating experience. By adopting standard processes they would be freed of their self-imposed complexity and be able to focus on work that was truly innovative.

Notwithstanding the difficulties, there is much that can be done—and must be done—to standardize processes if the goal of harmonization is to be achieved. With customers and suppliers alike, you need to be flexible and reactive, willing to go the extra mile to find a mutually acceptable solution.

At W. W. Grainger, Inc., which provides industrial maintenance, repair, and operating supplies, finding a standardized search mechanism for its customers was a crucial task.

Customers tend to be in a hurry when they sign on to Grainger.com because they are looking for a fast solution to a business problem—replacing a broken part, say—among the company's 500,000 products. Any number of products might help, but which are the best for the purpose?

There are a variety of potential standardized designs for that process. The most popular among such standardized processes is to have customers first click on the category of product they seek, such as motors. Then they get to choose the particular product, and then the horsepower, and then the RPMs. In other words, they keep narrowing down until they find what they want.

Just one problem with that standard: Grainger customers won't live in that world. They want something entirely different, and far simpler. They want to see an image of the right product on their screen with all the specifications they need within three clicks of their mouse.

The way Grainger has arranged it, customers can type in something like "I want a GE 5 horsepower or 30 horsepower or 3,450 RPM motor," and the motor and specifications will pop up along with a box enabling them to order it instantly. Grainger has thus standardized its product presentation process to better harmonize with its customers' procurement processes.

There are limits to how far cross-boundary standardization can be taken. You certainly don't want to standardize every aspect of a creative process, for example, but you do want to standardize enough to make sure that more of your organization's energy goes into innovation and real customer service and less into coping with a variety of different process styles, equipment, and software.

By the same token, although process standardization becomes more important as a company expands geographically, the company must also to some degree accommodate local customs in local markets. But caution is in order: If local demands are allowed to dominate process design, it will eventually lead to chaos and bring a company to a screeching halt.

The lack of standardized practices was wreaking havoc between suppliers and customers in the printing industry before R. R. Donnelley & Sons, introduced in Chapter 2, went on a three-year crusade to establish them. "In the past," said Donnelley senior vice president Tim Stratman in a recent speech, "publishers, retailers, and merchandisers were spending millions on paper without having anything in writing about what they were buying, beyond a No. 5 coated sheet. They were guaranteed nothing about roll diameter, nothing about delivery."

As a result, when the paper arrived at the printer to be turned into books or magazines, it was often late or the wrong width or the wrong finish. Printers would have to have huge inventories of paper at hand to make sure orders could be fulfilled.

Donnelley's move was simple in concept, harder to execute. But it suggested that the industry standardize on the widths and diameters of paper rolls. Now, with details clearly specified on orders, paper is more interchangeable, inventories have been reduced, and timely delivery is more likely. As part of the process, customers also send Donnelley copies of order acknowledgments, and as a result, said Stratman, "We're catching mistakes before they happen."

This kind of compatibility and standardization of processes by a few companies will eventually lead to the standardization of processes across industries. You may recall, from our previous discussion, that Solectron, Inc., is engaged in such an industry-wide effort. It is part of a Web-based network of companies that are creating processes to improve supply chain connections. The network has developed a common language that enables companies whose systems are incompatible to communicate effectively. That kind of patch suffices initially but will eventually give way to the next, X-engineered generation of processes and systems in which real standardization is the rule.

Here are some questions to help you think about standardization.

- What areas of my technology infrastructure must be standardized in order for information to move easily within my company and between my customers and suppliers?

- What information standards must I develop to meet the pull of customers? What are my customers' expectations about the information they receive or access?

- What are the processes that are common in my industry and where could efficiency be improved through standardization?

- Where does redundant work occur and where could common processes be shared?

Assign Responsibility

Harmonizing isn't just about making nice—it is about clearly establishing who is responsible for what in the design and operation of processes. Every successful relationship, personal or business, includes a willingness to assign and/or accept responsibility for one or another facet of the relationship.

To be sure, nowadays it is usually a buyer's market. If you want to keep a footloose customer, it may be necessary to make the lion's share of adjustments. That is what customer pull is all about. Yet, when customers can be shown distinct and substantial advantages in adapting to their suppliers' processes, they may be more than willing to adapt.

Inventory, for example, is often a bone of contention between suppliers and manufacturers and between manufacturers and dealers. How much of which products are to be inventoried? Where is it to be kept? Who will be responsible for it?

X-engineering suggests ways to answer those questions, harmonizing processes to get the right product to the right customer at the right time—while minimizing the capital invested in inventory.

Like the rest of the auto industry in the mid-90s, Honda

Motor Co., Ltd. was "pushing" cars at its customers—basing its production numbers on a ballpark estimate of demand and, with fingers crossed, shipping the autos out to dealers. Dealers had no real say in the cars they received, and had to wait at least four months to get a car that was made to the customer's order. Then, in 1996, American Honda, based in Torrance, California, attacked the lag time by creating a computerized, networked supply chain.

Honda's Market Oriented Vehicle Environment (MOVE) project has let everyone in the chain, from headquarters to assembly plants to dealers, collaborate in speeding up the process. Using the network, Honda's 1,300 dealers get a chance to review the company's monthly suggestions of what they might order. They can modify the list based on current demand in their territory, for instance, asking for fewer black Accord sedans and more red SUVs with sunroofs. It is the dealers' responsibility to understand the demands of their local markets. Honda uses this market data to generate production orders, with MOVE software calculating the most efficient way to distribute the load among its seven U.S. plants.

The system, completed in October 2000, now matches 95 percent of dealers' requests for cars. In addition, it has cut lead time on customers' orders for cars built to their specifications from 120 days to between 30 and 60 days. Eventually, Honda aims to sell all of its cars to the customer's order, just as Dell sells computers, with the delivery time cut to a matter of a few days.

In X-engineering terms, Honda has applied technology to develop better processes with clearly assigned responsibilities. By bringing all relevant parties to the table, by harmonizing its inventory-related processes with those of its dealers, the company and its network of dealers are better able to deliver product where it is needed.

Here are some questions to ask when dealing with assigning responsibilities.

- Of all the parties at the table, who has the best capabilities to manage a process?

- How will the capabilities of different organizations be utilized in joint processes?

- Do all the parties understand their responsibilities? Have they been clearly assigned?

- How will you know when someone isn't doing his job?

Make Processes Transparent

There is no way that partners in a supply chain can be truly connected unless most of their processes are transparent—that is, capable of being viewed not only by the partners but by all the other stakeholders in the enterprise. In the X-engineered world, information is to be shared; only the most proprietary of processes remain inviolate. It is the perfect formula for achieving harmonized processes.

Once again, Cisco has shown the way.

Since nearly every one of Cisco's processes is online and the company relies on the Internet to do just about everything, most of Cisco's operations are fully transparent. Whatever this costs in terms of corporate security is deemed worth the benefits of connecting Cisco's far-flung empire, coordinating plans, bringing in new employees and acquisitions with no fuss, communicating with customers and suppliers, and actually producing goods efficiently and on time. It is a central credo of Peter Solvik, chief information officer, that this level of transparency is essential to build and maintain a rapidly growing high-tech company.

On Cisco's CCO Web site, all information about the status of customers' orders is available to the company's sales force, direct customers, and sales partners. This includes shipment dates, backlog status reports, line-item details about each product on order, addresses, and order shipment status.

Cisco's corporate intranet, Cisco Employee Communication (CEC), is dynamic, transparent, and collaborative. Executives and managers announce new acquisitions and make staff announcements. Chefs post daily menus. One-quarter of the content comes directly from employees, who post news or hold discussions online. Employees worldwide communicate in proprietary newsgroups and "break rooms," where they can discuss company plans, share work techniques or technological improvements, and just gossip.

There is always the risk that some information a company wants to keep to itself will reach the outside, especially if it is made broadly available on its intranet. But this risk must be balanced against the benefits of a fully knowledgeable workforce—one that is aware of everything from how a product is made to how the company is performing.

Transparency and openness are consistent with two beliefs that underlie X-engineering. The first: People will take better care of themselves at less cost to the company when given access to company processes such as benefits administration and travel approval and reimbursement. The second: People will do the right thing for both customers and the company when they are given the right information. As a result, transparent, X-engineered processes can reduce corporate oversight and eliminate unnecessary controls.

Those basic beliefs also apply to customers and employees of supplier companies as well as internal people. The whole point of harmonizing your organization's processes with those of your customers and partners is to allow the people in all of these organizations to understand each other's needs and preferences and outlooks.

There may be only two questions to ask yourself about transparency: Am I protecting processes that aren't unique, and am I closed about information for which it would be better to be open? Remember, X-engineering changes the rule of protect and defend to one of be open and engage.

Degrees of Harmonization

Once you have selected the processes you want to harmonize, you must decide how far to go in integrating those processes with those of other companies or individuals. In other words, you need to determine what degree of harmonization you will attempt. In the paragraphs ahead, I describe three degrees of harmonization, starting with the least sophisticated.

OPENNESS

I have already described the importance of making your processes transparent. In the early stages of harmonization, this simply means that you open up and let customers and suppliers see how you operate. They may or may not connect as they wish. You do not seek to negotiate any joint process change with them.

Many companies are experimenting with openness. For example, most companies now post job opportunities on the Web together with lots of information about the company. Jobs are described in detail, which often enables you to gain real insight into the company's culture and management style.

Most major companies have also posted a catalog of their products on the Internet. This is the first step in opening up a selling process. They have by no means harmonized their processes with the buying processes of their customers. But this first act of transparency does force a company to clean up the descriptions of its products and services, no easy task for organizations that have thousands of product offerings. Just getting to an internal standard for product codes can be a challenge.

Openness is an early step in any form of harmonization, but it must go beyond the simple electronic dissemination of information. It must reveal how you operate. Companies hesitate to take that step in part because they do not want outsiders to see how weak and broken their internal processes really are. The more frequent reason given is the presumed proprietary nature of their processes.

In fact, as I noted earlier, there are few processes that will be unique to your operation. And even some of those may be safely revealed if you believe that your competitors cannot easily replicate what you are doing.

There is, of course, an additional benefit to improving your own operations and becoming more open: You can use the quality of your processes as a selling tool—with both customers and suppliers.

MUTUALITY

In mutuality, the second level of harmonization, the processes of two or more companies or customers become dependent on each other. The parties will not have actively negotiated any process changes across their organizational boundaries, but they will have developed some implicit expectations. The important characteristics of this stage of harmonization are predictability, consistency, and reliability. Customers will expect you to be open for business when they need you and will count on your doing business with them as you have in the past.

That may not be as easy as you think. It goes far beyond electronically operating a Web site 24 hours a day, 7 days a week. I paid a visit recently to a dealer in used and rare books, whose shop is located in a large, old house. I often stop by on a Saturday afternoon. I noticed that he had reduced his retail selling space. "Are you shrinking your business?" I asked. "Not at all," he responded. "My business is bigger and better than ever. I'm selling most of my books over the Internet."

Had the Internet made his job easier? No way. "See all these rooms," he said. "They're filled with computers and shipping boxes. Business is good. But I work harder now."

Courtesy of his Web site, the dealer and his customers were learning to do business with each other in a new way. His customers now depended on him not just to keep regular store hours but to be available 24/7, and they also expected him to deliver the books they purchased so they would not have to carry them out.

Customers of large companies have the same kind of expectations, and predictability and consistency is especially critical in business-to-business transactions. For example, many companies now make significant purchases through Internet auctions. I recently observed one such transaction in which a large bank bought $2 million worth of envelopes. Regular customers like this bank expect auction sites and the producers who sell through them to be there when they need them, to practice a consistent business protocol, and to provide reliable service and products. There are no long-term deals or even negotiations between sellers, buyers, and intermediaries at this level of harmonizing sophistication, but it does lead directly to process standardization.

INTEROPERABILITY

Many large companies have reached this degree of harmonization by means of what is commonly known as supply chain management. A company harmonizes its processes with those of its suppliers to make sure that materials or products are delivered when needed. In the automotive industry, the Ford Motor Company was a pioneer in this area. More than 10 years ago, the corporation began opening up to its suppliers of truck components, giving them production schedules and requiring that parts be delivered to its production lines as trucks were being manufactured. Other companies, such as Wal-Mart Stores, have taken supply chain management a further step, requiring their large suppliers to maintain the inventory in their stores. In Wal-Mart's case, that required the customer and its suppliers to develop a deep understanding of each other's processes. In most such cases, though, the customer simply demanded that suppliers adjust their processes to match its own—take it or leave it.

Interoperability requires a much more active negotiation between the parties of jointly shared processes. Solectron's relationship with its customers is a case in point. You will recall that the two parties share a single process to assure quality, and that there are shared design and engineering processes. It is difficult at times to distinguish who works for which company.

It is at this level of harmonization that companies get truly serious about process. There is active negotiation in which the parties define their individual versions of a particular process and the changes necessary to create a truly open process. Employees are chosen to take responsibility for each shared process, and metrics are developed for measuring the performance of the process. (You will see several examples of this kind of negotiation in subsequent chapters.)

Harmonization and Cannibalization

It may seem strange to consider the ideas of harmonization and cannibalization at the same time. This will be particularly unsettling to marketing executives who like to carefully segment their markets, usually by customer type. In an orderly world, services and products are designed to meet the needs of specific customer sets. But when you X-engineer and go to market through electronic channels, that orderly world gets turned on its head.

The reason is simple: Everyone gets to see what you have to offer, your price, and your terms. And everyone will want the best product, with the most service, at the lowest price. Your smallest customers will demand everything that you offer to your largest customers. The pressure will be on to reduce costs and improve speed and quality in order to meet this demand.

X-engineered processes will help you meet that crisis, but they will take their toll on existing products and sales channels. Inevitably, the newcomer products and channels will steal from or even consume their older counterparts. Such cannibalization should be an expected and accepted part of the continuous transformation required for success in today's business world.

When Lands' End, Inc., chairman David Dyer took his company online, he says, it was simply a logical way to extend his company's profitable mail-order business: "We did it because it perfectly leverages our infrastructure and is a more profitable model long-term." In any case, whether the customers bought by mail, phone, fax, or online, all the orders would be filled from the same giant warehouse in Dodgeville, Wisconsin.

But when Dyer made the move and cut Lands' End's catalog circulation by 18 percent to reduce costs, the result was a mini-disaster. Online shopping was cannibalizing the main event: Catalog sales of clothing for adults, the core of the business, dropped by 9 percent, and the stock price plummeted from $80 to $36.

Dyer plowed ahead, putting even more money and effort into the Web site to make it do things no catalog could match. One of its features let two friends shop together, each using her own computer. Another showed shoppers how to choose a swimsuit based on style and body shape and how to disguise what are somewhat coyly called "anxiety zones." Some 400 phone operators were trained as personal shoppers to guide visitors through the site, answering questions by phone or instant messaging and pushing Web pages for specific items.

The year after the new changes went into effect, Lands' End doubled its online sales to $138 million, 11 percent of total revenues. A fifth of the company's online customers last year were new to Lands' End—and many were younger than its core demographic group of 35-to-54-year-olds. Cannibalization had turned into finding new markets.

"We don't care how we get the sale, as long as we get it," Dyer says. "Cannibalization is good."

• • •

Harmony is always elusive, lost with a single wrong note. Yet, all managers must recognize, however, that the future belongs to companies that recognize its importance—the primacy of relationships in the networked marketplace. X-engineering is about optimizing relationships so that companies can tap the full sum of the intelligence and experience of all of the people in its network of customers, suppliers, and partners. To accomplish that goal, the processes in which these people participate must be arranged to work together smoothly both within an organization and between the organization and its customers, suppliers, and partners. When that happens, the ultimate form of harmonization will have been achieved, and success will follow.

Chapter 6

Using X-Engineering to Create Value

As we have seen, the X-engineered organization leverages its processes for maximum push and allows its customers maximum pull. At the intersection of those forces sits the business proposition—the promissory note in the form of a product or service that reflects your best effort to meet a customer's essential need.

Creating compelling and distinctive business propositions for your customers is a continuous process. It isn't something that you can get done, dust off your hands, and then relax to the soothing sound of cybercash flowing into your virtual bank account. Your competitors and customers alike are moving and changing much too fast for that.

This chapter describes and analyzes two organizations that have learned that lesson well. By constantly developing new propositions for their customers, by reacting to customer pull

90

and amending their process push, they have X-engineered an enviable track record for customer retention.

First, though, here is a rough outline of the steps they take along the path toward strong, flexible business propositions:

Step 1. *Continuously gather and digest essential information about your customers.*

In other words, develop the disciplines and processes for a true understanding of customer pull. As my friend Peter Drucker has put it, you have to know customers' "realities, situations, behaviors, expectations, and values."

We have already seen how Solectron Corporation and EMC Corporation achieve this in formal discovery meetings with customers. Similarly, if you have ever made a retail purchase from Amazon.com, you know how that company uses its technology to track and record your every whim and feed back new offers accordingly. Even the big industrial businesses, such as General Electric's Power Systems Division, are beginning to build institutional knowledge of customers' sophisticated needs.

Step 2. *Segment customers—but not too quickly.*

Segmentation isn't an exact science. Until you accumulate some authentic, unique knowledge about your customers, you should expect to provide all of them with an equal level of service. Any one company may not want or need everything you have to offer, but it will want to know what you have—and to make sure you aren't holding out or favoring other customers. Remember, the Internet makes everyone transparent.

When you have learned enough about your customers to do real segmentation, segment them by their expectations and values, not by their size, buying power, or profitability. Again, you should assume that all customers know what products and services you offer and that they will choose from among those offerings. As they begin to choose, you can begin to segment. Your long-range X-engineering goal, of course, is to eventually market to a customer segment of one, à la Amazon.com.

Step 3. *Determine the compelling proposition for each customer or customer set.*

Your distinctiveness could come from a single proposition or from a combination of propositions: the best price, the fastest delivery or development time, the best quality, the widest choice, the most innovation, or the best integration of products and services in your industry.

Once you know your customers' needs, expectations, and values, you may quickly be able to find compelling propositions. But more likely, you will have to search for opportunities.

Step 4. *Walk before you try to run.*

Sometimes companies try too hard to develop complete or sophisticated product offerings. That can present problems. The customer may not understand the complex proposition, or the company may not be able to execute it. Many customers just want something that works. Start with a simple proposition, get market traction, and then build from there. The Harvard Pilgrim Health Care, Inc. case, further discussed later in the chapter, illustrates the point.

Step 5. *Look for partners that will help.*

Here's where you should begin to consider choosing partners in delivering your proposition, how that proposition might be enhanced by relationships with other companies, and the form those relationships should take. (More on this in Chapter 8.)

Step 6. *Focus on process redesign.*

How can your processes and those of your partners be best designed to deliver a compelling customer proposition? Search for process opportunities—Chapter 7 tells how—and apply the lessons of harmonization that you learned in Chapter 5.

Step 7. *Constantly measure your performance through the eyes of your customers.*

"The most important time to ask seriously, 'What is our business?'" the legendary Peter Drucker once observed, "is when a company has been successful. Success always makes obsolete the very behavior that achieved it. It always creates its own and different problems." When you are doing very well, that is precisely the time to be most concerned about what comes next.

And one way to be constantly thinking about what comes next is to be constantly asking your customers whether your process push is meeting their pull. Companies such as Solectron and EMC lead the way in that regard, as do the two corporations that occupy the remainder of this chapter.

But before I begin those stories, let me add a word of caution on the importance of finding strong value propositions for your customers—propositions that separate you from your competitors. If you can't differentiate your offerings by what you sell or how you sell it, you will be forced to differentiate by how much you sell it for—and that will mean selling at commodity prices. The case ahead illustrates that how you sell can create a new value proposition for your customers.

W. W. Grainger—The Quiet Giant

People don't pay much attention to companies like W. W. Grainger, Inc., until trouble arrives. The compressor breaks down, the escalator stops dead, the assembly line grinds to a halt. You don't have the parts you need to make the repairs—or you have the parts, but you don't have the right tools. What to do?

For 75 years people in that kind of trouble have been calling Grainger, the largest distributor of industrial supplies in the United States. The Chicago, Illinois–based company specializes in maintenance, repair, and operating supplies, known in the trade as MRO, and it is that industry's leader in sales ($5 billion in

2000) and size (580-plus branches in the United States, Canada, and Mexico). It is also a textbook case of X-engineering in action, especially when it comes to the propositions it offers its customers.

Graingers's core business is industrial equipment and products—what the company calls the concrete side of the MRO trade, as opposed to the carpet side, office supplies. From A-coils to Zip screws, Grainger carries more than 220,000 products for markets ranging from contractors to hotels, from manufacturers to hospitals. Not long ago, Wesley M. Clark, its president, identified the company's four "value drivers" as "cost-savings, time savings, reliability, and innovation." They are, Clark said, "how Grainger differentiates itself from the more than 100,000 local distributors we compete with, and why 2 million businesses bought from Grainger last year."

Before we take a closer look, here is a bit of background on Grainger's industry. The $300-billion-a-year MRO market is the most fragmented imaginable, with 95 percent of market share split among tens of thousands of small, mom-and-pop distributors. It was the genius of William W. Grainger, the founder, to recognize that a single company with many local branches could give customers the convenience of a nearby supply house—a friend in need—as well as a standardized product offering and economies of scale. That concept remains central; the company boasts that 80 percent of all U.S. businesses are within 20 minutes of one of its branches.

When he set up his first supply shop in 1927, however, Bill Grainger's proposition was more basic. He was dealing in motors then, and he wanted to give his customers an easy, quick way to choose among the motors available and get the one they wanted—a service the manufacturers themselves could not provide. To that end, he created an eight-page wholesale catalog of motors. It soon evolved into the Grainger CATALOG, the industry bible. In 2000 the company distributed more than 2 million copies of that year's CATALOG, which contained some 86,500 brand-name products, including 6,500 different motors.

Searching the huge tome, however, is no simple matter. So Grainger offers alternatives. In 1991 it became the first MRO company to put its catalog on CD-ROM as well as paper. The company caught on to the Internet in 1995, and a year later began offering the contents of the CATALOG—and more—over its Web site, Grainger.com, another MRO industry first. In 1999 Grainger organized a group of seven supplier companies to join forces in a new Web site, providing smaller customers, in particular, with one-stop shopping for everything from office supplies and safety equipment to electronic supplies and uniforms.

The new site, Orderzone.com, was to be a kind of department store where customers could find goods and services from varied suppliers in a single orderly place with a common cash register. Customers needed only one simple registration, one search engine, and one order form, and they got only one invoice. This may sound easy to do, but such capability requires extraordinary process harmonization. Just meshing the different catalogs to work together was a challenge.

Within a year, the company took another online step by merging OrderZone.com with Works.com, Inc., a business-to-business start-up with a focus on white-collar companies—the carpet side of the business—and a program that enables customers to automate their purchasing process. The two organizations neatly complemented each other. "Their marketing model was syndication," Grainger CEO Richard Keyser told me. "They tend to live inside big brands that people are used to going to, so they didn't have to spend all that marketing money. But they had virtually no leverage over the suppliers, and the easiest thing for Grainger and Orderzone to find was suppliers."

Grainger has also developed its online offerings for particular customer needs. The latest generation of the company's original Web site, Grainger.com offers customization features such as personal lists, real-time pricing, and order tracking. A Repair Parts Center on the site enables customers to search, view, and order repair parts. Another example of Grainger's innovation in technological solutions is FindMRO.com, a source that helps customers locate hard-to-find or seldom-purchased MRO products. Launched in 1999, FindMRO.com expands choices for Grainger's customers who need specific and often unique products to solve a problem.

These initiatives underscore Grainger's openness to channels, providing ways to to create new value propositions for its customers. Both Works.com and Material Logic are also good examples of what I will later describe as "Level 4 Participation"— bringing in many different kinds of companies to expand your customer proposition.

And even that commitment to X-engineering is only the beginning of Grainger's use of process and technology to boost its business propositions fails to cover the extent of its X-engineering solutions.

Now let's take a closer look at those propositions.

PRICE

The basic structure of W. W. Grainger, with its multiple branches and standardized product offerings, provided huge savings for such major companies as General Electric, The General Motors Corporation, and McDonald's Corporation, all of which are current customers. It meant that they could leverage their purchasing power, saving substantial sums on every item they bought from Grainger by means of contract purchasing. It was a proposition that could not be matched by the company's competitors, who maintain call centers and a few warehouses or have only a handful of stores.

Grainger enhances that advantage by adapting rapidly to each new twist and turn of e-commerce, providing still more cost savings for its customers. Some 40 cents of every dollar spent on MRO products goes for the purchasing process, and Grainger is using the Internet to help its customers reduce those costs. A recent example: When Weyerhaeuser, Inc., one of the largest timber and paper-products companies in the world, set out to automate its supplier processes through e-procurement systems, it was obvious that it should ask Grainger to help.

Grainger had seen the value the value of e-procurement early on and had become one of just a handful of suppliers connected to and integrated with the leading new e-procurement systems. So when Weyerhaeuser, already a customer, made its move to streamline its procurement process, Grainger was ready—and became Weyerhaeuser's major MRO e-business supplier.

The cost-savings from these new systems are substantial. Weyerhaeuser says that the average cost of processing an MRO order runs between $50 and $100. The company expects that for a routine purchase e-procurement will trim that number to less than $10.

Grainger.com and its various incarnations are also focused on cutting costs for customers by providing them with efficient procurement processes. In the case of OrderZone.com and now Works.com, for example, Grainger and seven vendors created the first digital marketplace to offer their wares, so that customers need only one simple registration, one search engine, and one order form, and they receive only one invoice. This may sound simple, but such capability requires an extraordinary process harmonization.

Grainger's own Internet-fed cost-savings have been impressive, and have helped it to keep its price proposition attractive. Orders received over the Internet, for example, are far less costly to process than those that come in over the telephone or by fax. You will not be surprised to learn that the company has offered its salespeople special incentives to get customers to shop on Grainger.com.

SPEED

In most businesses, corporate customers take pains to plan their purchases well in advance. Preparation is all. But in the case of the MRO business, the majority of purchases arise from a sudden, unexpected need. That means time is of the essence, and speed of response and delivery are primary considerations.

Thus Grainger's Internet search engine allows customers to quickly pinpoint the precise product they need simply by answering a few questions—instead of having to sift through the thousands of products that might potentially seem appropriate. Using Grainger.com, customers don't have to search for products through supply houses, choose a vendor, fill out an order form, and process the paperwork; having found what they want, all of that happens automatically with two clicks of a mouse. The order moves even faster because the customer takes over the order entry process, and Grainger in effect becomes the customer's warehouse.

And some of the special features of Grainger.com, such as customized product lists tailored to specific industries or even individual companies, save customers even more precious minutes on each order. So does the ease of registration and the single order form and invoice. Customers like the speed and convenience. Butler, for example, a toothbrush manufacturer in Chicago, places 99 percent of its Grainger orders at that site.

At the other end of the transaction, the company sends out some 11,000 packages an hour, primarily through United Parcel Service, Inc.—a supplier that Grainger sees as a full partner in its business and with whom it has harmonized it processes. Grainger's logistics systems get most online orders to customers within 24 hours.

QUALITY

For manufacturers, their quality proposition is centered on the actual, concrete products they make—the excellence of the raw materials, the level of workmanship, the perfection of the finish. For distributors such as Grainger, however, the quality issues are somewhat different.

To be sure, the quality of the products it distributes is an essential part of its customer proposition. It carries only branded products, not generic items. But another big part of Grainger's quality proposition is the level of information that accompanies those products.

It is part of the company's heritage that the products it offers, both catalog and online, are accompanied by photographs and detailed information—detailed enough so that a customer can make an intelligent decision. Generalized descriptions and generic products need not apply.

Accuracy is another key to quality in the MRO business, and Grainger is very nearly obsessive about it. "With Grainger, when you order it you know that the right product will be shipped to you," Wesley Clark told me, "and that when you get the paperwork, the invoices will be correct, and it makes it a very easy, very accurate transaction." The company's measure of "first pass yield"—the portion of orders that sail through the system without anyone having to intervene to correct some sort of error—has soared from less than 50 percent into the low 90s, and Clark is determined to get it above 95 percent.

Yet another quality element in the company's proposition is the tracking information that it offers to phone, fax, and online customers to gain after their purchases have been shipped. They can simply go to Grainger.com and find out just where in the transport process their goods can be found.

VARIETY

The variety proposition is and has always been a key part of Grainger's strategy and one of the most important ways that it has been able to achieve competitive advantage. No other MRO company can match the 220,000 product choices that Grainger its customers.

This diversity may seem almost chaotic, defying the need for standardization. For the MRO business, however, it is essential. The customers' assembly lines, for example, are most often a wild mix of tools and machines that have been put together over the years. When a part in a 20-year-old machine breaks down, finding a replacement and finding it fast can be a daunting task. With its electronic locating systems, Grainger can make the task look easy.

Each of its 580-odd branch stores has an inventory averaging $2 million of the most frequently ordered products ready for immediate pick-up or same-day delivery. Grainger's six huge zone distribution centers, which average 220,000 square feet, keep the branches supplied and also maintain the enormous inventories needed to supply orders for less frequently used items.

At each of these centers, Grainger has put in place comprehensive electronic databases that make it possible to start with a description, a brand name, or a manufacturer's model number and quickly find the item ordered.

All told, Grainger is a fine example of a company that has been constantly developing its business proposition, pushing on many of the traditional values that its customers want: price, speed, quality, and variety. It has done this by pioneering the integration of its processes with those of its customers and a group of complementary supplier companies that could significantly add to Grainger's original propositions. Now it is enlisting its competitors as partners to X-engineer even more value for its customers.

To orchestrate all this has been no mean feat. But one thing in Grainger's favor is that most customers pretty much want the same thing of the MRO industry. Customer pull is relatively easy to discover. Not so in the health care industry, as the next case history demonstrates all too well.

Harvard Pilgrim Health Care—Center of the Storm

Imagine running a business in which all your customers wanted something different—in X-engineering terms, they were all pulling in a different direction. That is the condition that most organizations in the health care industry experience, and it applies in spades to such health maintenance organizations as Harvard Pilgrim Health Care, the HMO you met in Chapter 1.

The practice and business of medicine used to be a lot simpler. When you got sick, you saw a doctor. You went to the hospital if you were really ill. Either you or an insurance company paid the bills. Doctors wanted to cure their patients, and hospitals wanted to help.

That goal of doctors and hospitals—to care for patients and to save lives—is about the only element in health care that has stayed constant. Today, however, doctors complain that the practice of medicine is unduly constrained by managed care and that information technology, for the most part, makes their lives more complex, not easier. They see lots of useless work getting in the way of delivering good care—and when they do deliver care, they experience long delays in getting paid for it.

Hospitals and even large hospital systems have similar complaints, but their problems are more acute. Rising costs—much of them attributable to new treatments and technologies and to the complexity of the health care system itself—now conspire with inadequate reimbursements from government agencies and insurers to make many hospitals in the United States unprofitable. Many balance their books through gifts or income from endowments. Their condition is becoming critical.

Health-insurance companies struggle to control costs while providing adequate coverage. Employers complain that their insurance premiums are too high, while they still want to be sure that their employees are well cared for. It will be a challenge to give everyone what he wants.

And patients? They complain about the complexity of navigating through the system. But for the most part, if they are a member of an HMO or have other health care insurance, they get good care. That's principally because health care providers—doctors, nurses, hospitals, and technicians—remain dedicated to the work of improving the human condition, curing illnesses, and saving lives. It is hard to find a more inspiring proposition.

Harvard Pilgrim had its start in 1969 as the independent, nonprofit Harvard Community Health Plan (HCHP). Dr. Robert H. Ebert, the dean of Harvard Medical School, and his colleagues recognized that all parties to the health care business would need help in managing their way to the best care. HCHP originally operated on the "staff" model, controlling and delivering care directly through its own medical teams. It quickly developed a national reputation for its clinical expertise.

In 1995 HCHP merged with Pilgrim Health Care to become Harvard Pilgrim. The two organizations seemed to have complementary strengths. HCHP had a great group practice and its clinical expertise; Pilgrim was known for customer service and high member satisfaction. Then in 1997 Harvard Pilgrim spun out its group practice as an independent unit known as Harvard Vanguard. Harvard Pilgrim would now focus more on the management than on the provider side of the business.

Charlie Baker began his affiliation with Harvard Pilgrim as the chief executive officer of the Harvard Pilgrim group practice in the fall of 1998 but moved in the summer of 1999 to become the CEO of Harvard Pilgrim to help integrate the two very different cultures of Harvard and Pilgrim. Like his predecessors, Baker had a strong commitment to making managed health care work.

But Baker soon found that his problems were not just cultural. Harvard Pilgrim's processes were broken, so broken, as mentioned in Chapter 1, that it took months before the organization discovered how deep its problems were. Its process and information infrastructure was creaking under the weight of the merger, which was never fully implemented. HCHP and PHC continued to operate as relatively independent companies under a corporate umbrella long after the merger was completed. This created tremendous duplication and complexity. For example, fifty-five different information systems were in operation, producing conflicting and inaccurate data. Harvard Pilgrim had a hard time identifying its members and pinpointing its costs, much less establishing realistic prices for its services.

"If you are in the health insurance business, your data better be damn good," Baker says, "because you're using that data to make decisions that are going to impact your company 6, 12, and 18 months from now. If you don't have full faith in the comprehensiveness and precision of the data you're using, you're taking some huge and unacceptable risks."

Those risks led Harvard Pilgrim to the brink of bankruptcy, but Baker and his colleagues fought their way back. They followed the dictates of the first step that I described in the introduction to this chapter: Develop in-depth information about your customers. Then, in the words of step 6, they "focused on process redesign," repairing their processes and building a new information systems infrastructure.

They evolved a larger ambition as well: to develop a fix for the health care system as a whole, responding to all the ills its "customers" experience. Those customers include patients ("members" in Harvard Pilgrim parlance), doctors, hospitals, insurers, HMOs, and employers. The task is daunting. But Harvard Pilgrim is following an important X-engineering principle: Start small, get market traction, and build from there. Or, as step 4 would have it, "walk before you try to run."

Its first move was a service called HPHConnect. The business proposition: Give employers and members the ability to do simple and secure transactions over the Internet. Employers can use the Internet to enroll and un-enroll their employees and dependants; review, verify, and approve their employees' online enrollment data; and manage their employee roster and reconcile it with their payroll information and monthly premium bills.

Employees or members can enroll electronically; they can select a primary care physician based on search criteria that they choose, such as language, gender, or location; they can enter demographic information for themselves and their family members; they can review and approve any data before it is sent to Harvard Pilgrim; and they can review their specific benefits information.

Simple stuff, you say. You're right. But just having an accurate roster of members is a boon that many HMOs don't enjoy. With accurate and accessible information, Harvard Pilgrim is building the foundation for more sophisticated services, such as electronic bill presentment and payment capabilities for its providers and electronic claims inquiry and claims submission for employee members. And now Charlie Baker has the information he needs to do intelligent pricing.

As Harvard Pilgrim has moved out with HPHConnect, the customer pull has been strong. As of this writing, 1,200 employers representing almost 300,000 members are using the service, and over 200 providers groups representing over 5,000 providers are HPHConnected. Providers using HPHConnect are now conducting over 70,000 member eligibility and claims status checks per week with HPHC, using this Web-based tool. Connectivity is the ultimate proposition for Harvard Pilgrim's many varied customers. Once connected, they will be able to eliminate the redundant systems that plague the industry—the refiling of forms and the double and triple entry of data. Patients, information, and payments should move through the system with ease.

But Harvard Pilgrim isn't waiting for nirvana. It's moving on other fronts in addition to HPHConnect. Its case managers are now connected to an Internet-based case management system that allows instant access to medical records. The system enables case managers to assist members in getting the right help.

Not long ago, a Harvard Pilgrim member showed up in the emergency room of a Boston hospital with acute abdominal pains. While in the ER, he suffered a seizure, which triggered a full neurological work-up—costly in time for the patient and in dollars for the hospital and Harvard Pilgrim. Harvard Pilgrim's case manager was alerted as the work-up began and called up the member's records. The records indicated a medical history that might explain the condition. With that information, the hospital's clinicians changed the course of treatment, the member's problems were immediately diagnosed, and he was treated and released in about half the time that the whole process would otherwise have taken. It was a shining example of step 3: *Determine the compelling proposition for each customer.* If you have ever waited in pain in an emergency room, you will know how compelling a value good case management can be.

Harvard Pilgrim has also made medical-management tools directly available to members over the Internet. Here's an excerpt from a report on these tools by Charlie Baker.

We now have about six months of feedback on MyDiabetes, our self-help service available through harvard.pilgrim.org, and it's very, very positive. Members are using our glucose monitoring tools to keep track of how they're doing, and many are granting us permission to share their results with HPHC case managers electronically. If someone's results fall below the comfort zone, automatic electronic notification is sent to all of the appropriate clinicians. We also make a great deal of instructional and clinical information about diabetes available to them, and many take full advantage of this. Members are telling us that they're having more success managing their blood glucose levels now than at any time before. It's giving them hope—and it's working.

Notice that this whole process reflects step 7: *Constantly measure your performance through the eyes of your customers.* Baker and his colleagues have a great ambition for Harvard Pilgrim. It's visible and palpable. Get the complexity out of the management of health care and re-direct the 35 cents of every health care dollar that is spent on administration back into delivering great care. That's a proposition that anyone would love.

● ● ●

Grainger and Harvard Pilgrim are two very different kinds of enterprises, but they have much in common in the way they have practiced X-engineering. In both cases, it started modestly, but with great ambition. It has been continuous and shows no sign of stopping.

While reducing costs is an imperative for both organizations, at least as much energy is put into processes that deliver value in other ways for their customers. In the chapter just ahead, I suggest how to search for X-engineering opportunities that could deliver compelling customer propositions.

Chapter 7

Where to Mark the *X*

In a year 2000 study of 1,200 companies in the United States and Europe by a team from the University of Texas, the researchers found that 74 percent of the companies provided basic product information online—seemingly a high proportion. But there were wide disparities in their online operations. Only 55 percent offered customized service options, only 44 percent notified customers of their order status, and only 14 percent shared production information with suppliers.

The researchers also compared the respondent companies' Internet integration with their financial results. They concluded that the more a company had integrated the Internet into its operations, the more financially successful it was, measured by revenue per employee, gross profit margin, and return on invested capital. Truth be told, most companies will first use the Internet and apply X-engineering to achieve efficiencies, typically to reduce costs and speed service. Eventually, they may move on to focus on developing more sophisticated customer value propositions. As discussed in the previous chapter, you can discover some of these propositions by learning more about what your customers value and expect. But you can also find opportunities for X-engineering by closely examining your own operations and the operations of your customers and suppliers. Straightforward searches help: Find out where costs lie, where breakdowns occur, and where early decisions are made that can prejudice the outcome of a process. This chapter suggests where to look.

In general, I have found that managers find openings for X-engineering in two ways: Either they are driven to search by the necessity to cut costs or they are inspired to deliver more value to their customers. That is the way managers think. So I suggest that in looking for X-engineering opportunities, you go with the flow.

The cost and value approaches are not mutually exclusive. In fact, the most impressive results are achieved when both courses are pursued simultaneously. To do that, you must look for process and harmonization opportunities that will dramatically improve your business performance while at the same time creating more value for your customers. Let's look more closely at the two kinds of opportunity.

Cost Opportunities

It is becoming ever more obvious that no matter what else is included in your business proposition, if you are going to compete in today's demanding business climate you must be a low-cost producer. That means learning precisely how your company's money is spent and where its assets are concentrated. And your efforts should extend beyond your own corporate boundaries to encompass the entire supply chain. In this cost-cutting process there are great opportunities for X-engineering.

To begin with, recognize that your costs are not always what you think them to be, and that you may not be associating the right costs with the right activities. Look in detail at the real cost of capital and the costs of operations—both yours and your customers'. You may be surprised at your shared inefficiencies.

For example, inventory reduction has been one of X-engineering's most visible targets. Inventory sits in warehouses or in storage yards depreciating in value—and the higher the technology component of a product, the faster its value melts. The game of the last few years has been to get someone else to keep and own inventory until you or your customer needs it. But after the concept of "just-in-time" was developed, the questions of "on whose time" and "on whose nickel" inventory is kept still had to be negotiated between buyers and sellers, and someone would come out losing.

X-engineering's objective is to reduce total inventory for all parties while increasing the response times and service levels that a customer experiences. As described in Chapter 4, Michael Dell has demonstrated how to build computers to order, with ever shorter delivery times and ever lower costs. He has not only reduced his own costs but also those of his suppliers, and thus the total cost to the final customer.

The benefits of total inventory reduction and a build-to-order service can be enormous. For example, the U.S.-based automobile industry maintains billions in inventory in plant or on dealers' lots. This inventory depreciates dramatically over time. Since most customers still want to test-drive the model they are thinking of buying, it will never be possible to eliminate that inventory altogether. But if it could be cut by 90 percent, costs to everyone in the automotive supply chain could be reduced dramatically.

Cutting operating costs can be more challenging than spotting large chunks of depreciating assets. That's because excess operating costs, unlike physical assets, are more difficult to see. Costs aren't always associated with activities. They can be "marbled" into operations, just as fat is marbled into a steak. (I must credit my old partner, Mike Hammer, with that metaphor.) One technique that you may want to consider to determine where real costs lie is activity-based costing. You will see this technique applied in the Owens & Minor case later in this chapter.

You also have to look broadly when your objective is to cut costs. For example, the average cost of handling raw materials in a manufacturing process is 4 to 10 times the purchase price of those materials. That means that if you focus your X-engineering work solely on procurement, you will miss most of the opportunity for cost improvement. You cannot stop with fixing procurement. You must go further to examine all the processes linked to procurement, including inspection, inventory management and logistics, recycling, environmental health and safety reporting, and liability avoidance, among others. Then you can start looking for inefficiencies in the actual manufacturing process.

And to drive home an earlier point: Since X-engineering is primarily about business-to-business process performance, it is just not your own company's costs that matter. What matters is total landed costs—the total cost of your product or service in the hands of your customer. It may seem like magic, but if you are good at following the money and redesigning processes along the whole supply chain, it is possible to reduce total landed costs to your customer and increase your own profit at the same time.

Also remember the more processes you include in your search for X-engineering opportunities, the greater your potential for business performance improvement—but the greater the complexity and challenge of change.

Value Opportunities

The second route to X-engineering begins with a customer. As you get to understand the customer pull—what customers value and what they expect—you will become quicker and better at developing customer value propositions. But before opportunities become visible, you might begin by charting breakdowns. You may be surprised by the positive insights gained from studying operations that produce negative results, especially those affecting customers.

Begin by recognizing that your customers know more than you do about the problems they are having with your products or services. You need their input if you are to get to the bottom of their problems. A study of one group of companies, for example, found that fully 40 percent of the invoices sent to their customers were dead wrong. But the errors did not originate in the billing departments. The companies provided complex products and services, and the errors actually stemmed from intricacies that weren't properly communicated to the billers.

Processes such as billing and accounts receivable don't receive much attention from senior managers unless cash becomes a problem. These areas aren't very exciting, but they cause real problems for customers when breakdowns occur. To rework inaccurate invoices and chase down errors can take a lot of time and create a lot of pain. But it is well worthwhile: There is opportunity in these processes to reduce the operating costs of all participants while improving the service proposition to customers.

If your processes are properly tuned to customer pull, you can tell when breakdowns with customers occur and how your processes need to be redesigned to avoid these breakdowns.

Breakdowns have always been more visible to a company's customers than to its executives. But now the Internet is accelerating the rate at which customers experience problems and learn about their colleagues' bad experiences. Unless managers also find out more about what's going on, they will be helpless to deal with increasingly unhappy customers.

Chapter 3 described how Solectron's customers participated in a weekly performance review. This process immediately shines a spotlight on breakdowns—and, as a corollary, it is quickly followed by action to fix the cause of the failure. At Solectron, charting breakdowns, fixing the problem, and re-measuring performance is a closed-loop process.

But fixing processes to respond to breakdowns or poor performance will not usually go far enough to deliver a truly compelling new customer proposition. In order to achieve more, you will have to go deeper into understanding your customers' processes. I call that looking upstream—in both of your operations.

Case in Point—Owens & Minor

For a good example of applied X-engineering, both in reducing costs and adding value by serving customers' needs, consider Owens & Minor, Inc. With $3.5 billion in annual sales, it is a relatively small Fortune 500 company, but it is the leading U.S. distributor of medical and surgical supplies to hospital systems. And it is revolutionizing its industry by applying the principles of activity-based management (ABM).

O&M has long been in the technological forefront: It installed its first computerized order system back in 1954, the Jurassic age of computing. In 1990, still well ahead of the pack, the company embarked on an aggressive growth strategy with a commitment to technology and supply chain partnerships. The strategy was successful. As the new century approached, CEO G. Gilmer Minor III, whose great-grandfather co-founded the company in 1882, could boast that O&M was distributing 170,000 medical and surgical products through 45 distribution centers to 4,000 hospitals across the country. It was one of the largest distributors in the health industry, which was itself growing inexorably, and the future should have looked golden.

But there were snakes in this Eden; as Minor puts it, "We saw the world changing around us." As managed care swept the industry, hospitals came under enormous pressure to cut costs. They merged, consolidated, and formed buying groups to increase their market leverage, squeezing down distributors' already thin profit margins. They learned to buy their most expensive supplies direct from the makers, cutting distributors out of the loop and paying them only for high-volume, low-profit supplies. And the manufacturers added to the pressure by raising prices and shaving the discounts they had traditionally given distributors. When O&M raised its own prices by 1 percent across the board in 1995, some of its customers switched to other distributors. O&M chalked up a loss for the year of $11 million.

A basic roadblock to change was the cost-plus pricing system, standard in the health care industry for two decades. Distributors traditionally took a markup of 6 to 8 percent on the manufacturer's price, which was supposed to cover their costs and provide their profit. But as cost pressures grew, hospitals fought to cut inventories by demanding more frequent deliveries. Some converted to "stockless" operation, with just-in-time delivery so finely tuned that O&M was handing over boxes of sutures directly to operating rooms.

This added to O&M's costs not just by multiplying delivery trips but by requiring more inventory and extra handling of the supplies as pallets were unloaded and goods were repacked in smaller boxes. Managing inventories led to product returns, financing costs, and the special problem of making sure medical products were used before their expiration dates. And since hospitals felt free to hold payment for 90 days, the receivables had to be financed, too.

But O&M couldn't even track its own costs with any certainty. Its processes had developed haphazardly, with some clients getting more services than others. "We had gotten into some contracts where we underpriced the service because we didn't know what our costs were," recalls Jose Valderas, divisional vice president. "We knew what our total costs were to run our warehouse for all customers. However, we didn't understand how much it would cost to run one particular account, pick the orders in the fashion the account needed, make the number of deliveries they needed, and so on." What O&M had to do, he concluded, was "to separate the price of the box from the price to move the box."

It was to solve that problem that Director of Cost Management Michael Stefanic set up a pilot program in activity-based costing (ABC) at the distribution center at O&M headquarters in Savage, Maryland. It is a well-tested, scientific way to follow the money, attaching real costs to real processes. By paying attention to how employees actually divided their time among various processes and customers, he found that costs—and thus profitability—depended on a few key factors, most of them controlled by the customer. These included the type of service requested (e.g., traditional bulk deliveries versus a stockless system); the number of purchase orders per month; the number of lines in each order; the number of deliveries per week; whether the order came in by phone, fax, or electronically; and the interest cost of carrying inventory and receivables. This approach also gave O&M the opportunity to observe more closely the inefficiencies in its customers' processes.

Using that data, O&M made some progress in cutting its own

costs. But it had already been an efficient operation; the real problem was the straitjacket that cost-plus pricing and managed care had produced and the cost burdens imposed on O&M by its customers' poor processes.

Adding to the pressures, the manufacturers of medical equipment were also pushing for a more efficient supply chain. Their goal was to set up a continuous replenishment process, with a flow of information stretching from raw materials producers to the patient's bedside to ensure the smoothest possible operations. But here again, O&M was frustrated; given the hospitals' lack of attention to process, continuous replenishment was not an option any time soon.

The problems came to a head, and the beginnings of a solution emerged, in 1996. Ideal Health System had been using a rival distributor but announced that its $30 million annual business was now up for bids. In the past, the competitor had been able to underbid O&M because it was affiliated with a manufacturer and could discount those products. Valderas knew Ideal wasn't happy with that arrangement because its member hospitals would prefer more choice of product. But how low a bid would it take to get the contract, and how could he cover his costs?

He was studying the latest ABC report when the idea hit: O&M could abandon cost-plus pricing and convert to activity-based pricing, taking a markup of zero and charging for the services it actually performed. In that way, customers would see the actual costs of the processes associated with the services they were demanding.

Sizable risks were involved. Activity-based costing was a fairly new concept, difficult both to grasp and to implement. The health care industry was used to cost-plus pricing, which was built into the industry's financial and accounting structure, from budgeting to the incentive program. How could a distributor's fee be inserted in a hospital budget that didn't have a line for it? How could it be factored into transfer prices on products moving from one department to another? And fundamentally, how could Ideal—and other hospitals in turn—be persuaded that this whole approach wasn't just a fancy scheme to charge higher prices?

The challenge wasn't easy. But O&M found opportunity in following the money because it was looking to reduce hospitals' costs and improve their operations at the same time. Valderas and his colleagues had not merely listened for customers' complaints; they had perceived problems that the customers hadn't yet detected themselves.

In truth, the cost-plus system wasn't working well for the hospitals, either. As the ABC data showed, the system masked inefficiencies and costs that were built into the hospitals' operation. O&M's services were largely used to paper over problems that O&M had no power to cure. Even the expedients that the hospitals had found to cut their payments to distributors didn't come without a price. If they bought expensive goods direct from the makers, for instance, they had to buy more than they wanted and swallow the inventory cost. In forcing distributors to lower their margins, they thought they were getting bargains; but the distributors often found a way to raise the price of less conspicuous items, which a hospital would discover only after an audit two years later.

By following the money, hospitals could track their own costs, improve their own efficiency, and actually reduce their payments to O&M, while O&M would perform less service and earn more profit. In my terms, the total landed cost of the service would be sharply reduced, to everyone's benefit.

But O&M would have to be completely transparent about its costs—and swallowing hard, Gil Minor agreed. O&M opened its books, showing Ideal its detailed costs and its meager profit of less than 1 percent of revenues. Impressed with the distributor's forward thinking, flexibility, and dedication to customer service,

Ideal agreed to make the transition to a modified version of activity-based pricing.

For a long time, the whole concept was a hard sell for the rest of the industry. Early on, says Tim Gill, O&M's director of logistics and support services, there were only blank stares when he asked customers if they knew about activity-based management. O&M put on a series of educational seminars around the country to persuade hospitals that the new way would help their bottom lines. The company also figured out that the pitch worked better with financial officers, who could see the larger picture, than with the purchasing materials people who traditionally dealt with distributors.

Activity-based pricing also involved a continuous process of X-engineering. Over time, O&M developed an array of technological programs to implement activity-based pricing. There was WISDOM, Owens & Minor's Internet-based data mining tool that allows customers to mine their own purchasing datas held in Owens & Minor's vast data warehouse for trends and compliance. This innovative software program helps subscribing hospitals clearly identify and track the costs in a materials management system. In 2001, the company has followed with WISDOM 2, a program that could also track products bought not only through O&M but from other sources as well. Those programs, in turn, were incorporated into CostTrack, a three-step program that O&M uses with each client to make a baseline analysis of costs, find out what the system lacks, and provide services that will add value. One such service is OM Direct, an Internet-based purchasing system that lets buyers ascertain the availability of products, order goods for delivery to the distributor, manage their inventory with hand-held computers, and make better-informed decisions than ever before.

What O&M shows its customer, says Tim Gill, is "what you really need and what makes sense for you. Is there anything you're doing internally that we could probably do better for you, or are there any services that we're providing you that maybe you don't need?"

A customer who has been getting six deliveries a week, for instance, might decide to cut O&M's fee by $2,000 a week and get along with five deliveries. That marginal increase in inventory cost is more than offset by cutting the time the customer's own staff spends unpacking and handling goods. Another hospital might assess the costs of its own internal handling system and pay O&M a smaller sum to deliver goods to the point of use. O&M might install its own sophisticated materials handling system in a customer's warehouse, taking over inventory management and hiring some of the customer's former staffers to run the system.

All told, Gil Minor tells his clients, "This is the silver bullet." But he also warns them that it takes a lot of time and work to get the processes to fit. There is a learning curve of about one year before major results start coming, and many customers need continuing help from O&M to make the system work. But that produces another major benefit: As customers catch on to what the harmonized process can do for them, their relationship with O&M quickly changes from adversarial wariness to a new trust. "Once they see your costs, and say 'Hey, these guys are really trying to help,' that's when you really start seeing change," says Tim Gill. And when O&M applies its tools and techniques to the customers' processes, "We can give them information about their own operations that they never saw before."

At last count, 22 percent of O&M's business had been switched from cost-plus to activity-based pricing, accounting for $764 million worth of goods. Minor's goal was to reach 50 percent within three years. And the X-engineering will continue. In the next few years, O&M hopes to develop OM Direct into an Internet-based marketplace that connects with other marketplaces and lets customers buy goods from other distributors as well as from O&M.

In the long run, says Minor, the goal is "to make this whole ordering business seamless, from the point of use all the way back to the manufacturer's production line and then back through the supply chain." That's a long trip—but then, he has already gone a good part of the way. As a postscript to this story, O&M was named by *Information Week* as the leading business use of technology in *Information Week*'s 13th annual ranking of the top 500 companies. It was an early technology adopter in 1954 and continues its process and technology innovations.

● ● ●

As the O&M story illustrates, there are several principles to keep in mind as you look for opportunities to X-engineer your own business:

- Follow the money. Knowing the real costs of operating can provide you with great insight as to where process improvement opportunities might lie. But don't stop at your own costs. Look at your customers' total landed costs for your product and services. And find out what it costs your suppliers to deliver materials in the manner you have requested. Also look for opportunities to reduce capital expenditures by managing inventory differently or sharing ownership of fixed assets with your customers, suppliers, and partners.

- Go broad. Excess costs in operations and performance problems generally are not attributable to a single activity or even a single process. The broader your net, the more you will find. Look across your processes and the processes of your customers and suppliers. The further you go, the greater the opportunity and the greater the challenge.

119

- Know what your customers are going through. The French philosopher Simone Weil used to tell her students that when meeting a person they should not ask "How are you today?" but rather "What are you going through today?" Weil argued that it was the more authentic question.

    Similarly, it is better to ask about the authentic realities and challenges facing your customers than to ask about their immediate needs. You need to have an intimate knowledge of your customers' concerns, not just their buying history, to find business propositions that will work for them and for you.

- Chart breakdowns. Analyzing failure will give you some direct clues as to where you might improve your processes and business propositions. Talk to your customers directly and openly about problems as they occur. It will give you great insight as to customers' expectations and what they really value.

- Fish upstream. The cost of a product, service, or process is substantially determined in its design phase. That is true for you, your customers, and your suppliers. Look upstream with your customers and suppliers into their design processes and see where you can foster early harmonization.

    The farther back you go in the processes of your customers and suppliers, the more efficiency improvements and customer value you are likely to create.

Finally, in your search for X-engineering opportunities, let me suggest that you use a mix of optimism and realism. Pessimists need not apply for this work. They worry too much about breaking something or that their company or customers may never change.

But optimism is important in order to see opportunity. Realism grounds you in the scope of the task ahead, dispenses with the hubris around technology, and forces you to confront the limits of your own capabilities and partnerships that you will need to form. That's where thinking begins about who will participate with you in X-engineering, and that is the subject of the next chapter.

Chapter 8

How Many Boundaries
Will You Cross?

Ever since the British launched the East India Company, managers have believed that big is good. Success was defined as selling everything from whale oil to tea and traveling the world to trade in every port. After all, scale brings potential economies and the opportunity to seize ever more market share.

In the twentieth century, the General Motors Corporation demonstrated how to build the quintessential giant, vertically integrated, multi-divisional company. Like most businesses that wanted to grow, GM bulked up by organically building capacity and by buying other companies. GM's strategy was to have a product for every market and to own all the strategic capability required to deliver. But by late in the twentieth century, it became clear that building, buying, and owning all the resources required for scale was not always an advantage. Bulking up required capital and generally didn't create a very nimble company. In fact, in modern business history, General Electric may be the only company that has successfully grown in physical size, consistently provided good financial returns, and been a market leader.

The challenges of nimbleness and financial returns for larger companies have bolstered contemporary arguments that big is no longer good and that the future will belong to the small, fast, and nimble. Don't believe it. Scale and presence—at least virtual scale and presence—is critically important to operate in an Internet-enabled world. Your customers will expect you to deliver almost anything, anywhere, anytime, no matter how big or small you are. But let's get back, for a moment, to business history.

By the 1970s managers began to realize that they didn't have to own all the assets and capabilities needed to achieve scale. They also recognized that some companies could perform certain processes better and cheaper than their own, and the idea of outsourcing took hold. Companies began to outsource everything from information technology operations to building maintenance services. These were generally arms-length transactions that involved little or no cross-company process integration, and certainly no harmonization as I have described it.

About the same time, the idea of creating alliances with business partners became popular. The theory was that companies could join forces to achieve scale and market coverage that they could not easily win on their own. But, truth be told, almost all such business alliances have failed to reach their stated goals. For example, within the last five years, several joint ventures have been formed by major American and European telecommunications companies to provide large customers with global communications coverage from a single source. Almost all of these ventures now lie in a heap, victims of poor process designs, competing capabilities, fumbled execution, and inter-company cultural clashes. They are the antithesis of X-engineering.

X-engineering does, however, expand your choice for achieving scale to three alternatives: build, buy, or buddy. In more managerial terms, it requires that you ask two questions: Who should participate with you—including customers, suppliers, partners, and competitors—in the creation and delivery of your business proposition, and how far should you go in integrating your processes.

In the 1990s Eli Lilly and Company, the Indianapolis, Indiana-based pharmaceutical research and development company, found itself asking those questions. Should it go for scale by building or buying, or should it focus more narrowly on the parts of its business it did best and find partners to participate in the rest?

In this chapter, I analyze the company's decision to take the second road, creating not actual bulk but "virtual" scale through technology-enabled relationships that deeply integrate processes across multiple organizations. I will also discuss several other examples of companies that have chosen different levels of partnership to achieve both scale and competitive advantage.

When Lilly considered its prospects, it was well aware of some key trends. On the negative side, the pharmaceutical industry was being challenged by growing resistance to high medical costs on the part of government and business payers. Yet, the rising demand for new drugs was forcing the industry to take greater risks using ever more expensive tools, so that research-and-development costs were soaring toward $1 billion per drug.

On the positive side, the ongoing research into the human genome promised discoveries that would vastly increase the number of potential new drugs. The market for drugs was sure to grow with the graying of the population. And the growing public use of the Internet to access health information was speeding up the adoption of new drugs by physicians and consumers.

The industry, by and large, was convinced that the positives outweighed the negatives, and many of Lilly's competitors went on a spree of mergers and acquisitions to bulk up, not only for research and development but also for sales and marketing. Lilly, too, decided to concentrate on R&D and sales and marketing, hoping to speed up the invention of blockbuster products and get them to more—and more profitable—customers.

But it opted for a different approach. The company, despite its tradition of scientific and marketing independence, began looking for partners rather than companies to merge with or acquire. "We began to rid ourselves of our old not-invented-here and not-owned-here prejudices," Sidney Taurel, chairman, chief executive officer, and president, explained not long ago. "In their place, we set the goal of becoming our industry's best business partner."

To make that happen, and to lift productivity, Lilly embarked on a many-faceted X-engineering program to connect all the processes within its walls as well as those that crossed organizational boundaries. Basic operational processes were redesigned, and a new technology infrastructure was installed. Informal networks of employees with similar interests were encouraged; these so-called "communities of practice" promoted the sharing of expertise.

The company also set up databases of employees with special skills and knowledge that could be available to colleagues in need of help. A new system aided employees of Lilly and its partner companies in information searches. Lilly also set up an e-procurement program.

True to its intentions, the company has entered into more than 100 alliances and has cemented them with information-technology tools. A partnership database connects Lilly people to those allies, and the company has opened its network to some of its scientific partners so they can access data on clinical trials.

The all-pervasive role of information technology and the Internet in Lilly's reinvention inevitably led to changes both in its structure and in the relationships among its employees and managers and in its structure. Most important, the new technology flattened the hierarchical structure. Once the connections between employees were in place, the employees had access to information that let them solve many more problems and make many more decisions on their own, without constant reference to managers.

That was true on many levels. When a scientist hits a technical snag, for example, she no longer needs to inform her manager, who will then contact other managers in search of expert advice. She can simply look for the appropriate "community of practice" or check the database of experts or do some fast online research. Similarly, when a production person needs to check some figures or work out a schedule with a supplier or partner, he can deal directly and instantaneously online instead of having to go up and down traditional hierarchical channels.

One of the most dramatic structural changes is embodied in the so-called e.Lilly team. In the spring of the year 2000, Lilly's CEO, Taurel, convened a meeting of what he described as a group of "our highest-potential younger executives" and gave them a month to find new company uses for the Internet. Their report led to the creation of e.Lilly, a small, primarily virtual team of X-engineers. It operates outside the boundaries of the company's line structure as a kind of incubator unit reporting directly to Taurel.

Among other things, the team seeks to increase learning and the sharing of best practices across the enterprise. It rides herd on more than 100 existing e-business projects and has a role in 60 other programs. It directly manages 29 projects and ventures, internal and external, that are transforming the company's business model, including the operation of a venture fund of $50 million that invests in start-ups.

One of the team's projects seeks to establish an informal, Internet-connected network of tens of thousands of chemists and biologists around the world that could be tapped to help the company overcome technical roadblocks. Another aims at having medical professionals report the results of clinical trials directly and in real time over the Internet, avoiding the communication failures caused by illegible handwriting, misunderstood form entries, and lost paperwork.

Lilly has not neglected its second target area, sales and marketing. The company has multiplied its Internet connections with customers, particularly with patients and their families. It has more than 30 Web sites concerned with individual products or diseases.

Because of today's time pressures on physicians, a key customer segment for pharmaceutical firms, industry salespeople have an average of only two minutes to present their products. So Lilly is experimenting with new ways to reach and sell to physicians over the Internet.

And the benefits of e.Lilly have stretched well beyond research and development to the entire corporate culture. The incubator project has speeded up decision making and response time in general, encouraged risk-taking, and encouraged employees to get closer to customers. It is, in fact, a tribute to the structure-altering capacities of the Internet.

But Taurel expects that e.Lilly will be disbanded in 2005. "By that time," he says, "Lilly and e.Lilly will have become one."

Participation

A key decision managers must make in their quest for growth and competitiveness is the extent to which their company will participate with other organizations. How extensively will a company cross organizational boundaries to harmonize its processes with those of its customers, suppliers, and partners? How many different kinds of organizations does it want or need to involve in the redesign and X-engineering of its business and operations?

I have identified four different levels of participation that derive from the decision to begin X-engineering, either alone or in partnership with other organizations. Level 1 represents the least challenge and complexity. At this level, a company simply X-engineers its own internal processes. Levels 2, 3, and 4 progress successively to more and more complex scenarios in which a company's X-engineering programs include its customers, suppliers, partners, and even competitors. In Level 2 a company participates with one other type of organization; in Level 3 it participates with two different types of organizations, say, customers and suppliers; and in Level 4 it participates with three different types of organizations, such as customers, suppliers, and complementing partners.

As you consider each in turn, please observe that all these examples are drawn from so called "bricks and mortar" or "old economy" companies that are reinventing themselves. There is more than life left in their good bones.

Level 1

At this level, a company upgrades its own processes. The work is similar to traditional reengineering but focuses on the electronic tools that enable structural reforms. When a company progresses from reengineering to X-engineering its internal processes, it becomes a self-improver, sampling the new world and considering whether to go further. This is a natural progression: A company must get its own house in process and digital order before it can do more.

The following case studies of X-engineered internal processes are drawn from the experiences of two very different companies: retailer Saks, Inc., and high-tech product manufacturer Honeywell International Inc.

As you will see from the Saks example, early X-engineering

moves are often focused on improving customer-facing processes. Customers expect a consistent, high-quality experience when transacting business through electronic channels. As many of the lately deceased dot-coms learned, you can lose customers quickly if that experience fails. Level 1 X-engineering also prepares a company for the transparency that more aggressive X-engineering requires. If you are going to let others into your company, your operations have to look good.

SAKS, INC.

Saks operates more than 350 department stores in the United States under 10 different names, including the prestigious Saks Fifth Avenue. When the national retailer wanted to significantly upgrade its customer service operations and offer a consistent quality of service response across all its brands, it decided to develop a customer-relationship portal. This multimedia portal integrates customer queries from multiple channels including phone, fax, e-mail, and Web chat rooms into one system. It was inaugurated during the 2000 holiday season.

For Saks, it means that the company's customer service sites in Jackson, Mississippi, Aberdeen, Maryland, and Elmhurst, Illinois can route customer queries to the most appropriate service representative, no matter where they are located. Because the system can call up data about the customer who is calling, select customers can be routed to the best-trained agents for the fastest, most responsive service. This is the beginning of intelligent customer segmentation.

Without adding a single new staff member, the average response time for phone calls was slashed from 45 seconds to less than 8. The portal resulted in payroll savings of $750,000 annually at just one of Saks's customer service centers. The investment in process and technology change was considerable, but the improved service and savings have more than paid off.

HONEYWELL INTERNATIONAL INC.

Morristown, New Jersey–based Honeywell International Inc., had a seriously dysfunctional inventory-forecasting system. By the time the company decided which forecast to use—a process that typically took four to five weeks—the forecast was out of date and had an accuracy of only about 50 percent. As a result, Honeywell's inventory of finished goods was swelling up, creating an unnecessary expense. Honeywell wanted to cut the time it took to forecast inventory and increase the accuracy of the forecast.

The company also wanted its planning and purchasing processes to be better integrated. More specifically, its goals were to

- enable global demand planning

- plan demand daily rather than every three weeks

- allow real-time simulation to predict the impact of any proposed plan

- be able to report and query on any of three bases: business unit, product line, and geography

In the first six months after implementing its new processes and systems, Honeywell dramatically improved the internal coordination between its planners and buyers. The company has cut its work-in-progress inventory by $50 million and achieved an 80 percent accuracy rate in forecasting. In addition, it expects to eliminate another $150 million in excess inventory over the next two years.

This example involves more process change back into the operations of the company than the Saks example. Saks altered process change principally at the interface with customers. But both examples share a common characteristic: Neither of them asked anything more of their partners—customers or suppliers—than what they normally asked. That will change in Level 2 X-engineering, increasing the challenge of the X-engineering work and the payoff.

Level 2

At Level 2 of participation, companies X-engineer both their own processes and those of one other organization, whether it is a customer, supplier, or partner. These companies are typically powerful in their industry and so good at what they do that the other organization is ready and willing to go along. Such organizations quickly experience the benefits of X-engineering. Consider, for example, The Boeing Company.

THE BOEING COMPANY

The numbers are staggering: more than 190,000 employees, a product line that ranges from commercial jets to helicopters to satellites and missiles, and a physical plant that includes the largest building in the world. This giant, of course, is the Boeing Company, which with $51 billion in revenues in 2000 is the world's largest airplane builder.

As big as it is, Boeing has a vision of becoming a more nimble and faster-moving company. In the view of chief information officer Scott Griffin, a fast company beats a slow company every time. "The interesting issue for a big company is that when you're big, it is very hard to be fast," he says. "We want to be big and fast."

This appetite for change traces to an ominous trend: In 1990 the company delivered 527 new airplanes. In 1995 the number dropped to 257. The causes were production problems and fierce competition from European consortium Airbus Industries.

The production bottlenecks in turn traced to the stupefying array of options that Boeing's commercial aviation division offered its customers. Did anyone really need 100 different shades of white and 20,000 different galley and lavatory configurations on the 777? Boeing decided that it had to get the production process under control, and began a complete overhaul and rationalization of the assembly process. The aerospace industry loves acronyms, and Boeing came up with a tongue-twister for its reform: DCAC/MRM, for Define and Control Airplane Configuration/Manufacturing Resource Management.

The company also began an overhaul of its supply chain processes.

The first phase, designed to make the company leaner and faster, and more closely linked to its 22,000 suppliers, is a procurement program called e-Buy. "In giant companies," says e-Buy director Paul Pasquier, "paper tends to drive the processes and systems." By removing as much paper from the system as possible, Boeing aims to lower internal costs by 20 percent.

The e-Buy project involves some 8,000 Boeing purchasing agents who buy items ranging from pens and paper to airplane sub-assemblies. Pasquier's goal is to see his purchasing agents become a single team as Boeing moves all of its procurement online in 2001. He aims to cut the cycle time from a week to one day and raise inventory turnover from three to four times per year.

The centerpiece of e-Buy is an online marketplace for the aerospace industry called Exostar. Boeing's plan is to have 1,000 suppliers using Exostar by the end of 2001, especially those Pasquier refers to as high-volume suppliers. At first, suppliers will only need a Web browser to use Exostar initially, but Pasquier says Boeing will next integrate the suppliers' entire infrastructures to Exostar.

With that degree of harmonization, Boeing and its partners will experience even more benefits. Redundant and overlapping work will be eliminated, speed of transactions will improve, and errors will be reduced.

Level 3

At Level 3, X-engineering companies change their own processes along with those of two other kinds of organizations: customers, suppliers, or partners. The company that I have chosen to illustrate Level 3 is Intel Corporation. You have most probably read a lot about this company, but this description will underscore the complexity and challenge of Intel's ambition as well as the breadth and scope of its achievement.

INTEL CORPORATION.

"Only the paranoid survive," Intel chairman Andy Grove once famously said. If that was true for Grove, it is even more so for his successor, Craig Barrett. Since Barrett took over the helm at Intel as president in 1997 and CEO in 1998, he has seen the personal-computer market level off and the Internet economy implode. Intel's sales have plummeted, and the company recently announced that it would eliminate 5,000 jobs.

Although Barrett has reallocated resources to focus on the company's core chip business and scaled back some of Intel's Internet services initiatives, he remains convinced that this reduction is temporary. He is also committed to the Internet economy. "We expect that our networking and communications businesses will grow even faster than our old core business," he says. "It's a huge growth opportunity."

Intel recognized early on that the business-to-business part of the Internet was where the action was. "Being an Internet company meant turning ourselves into a 100 percent e-business front to back," says Barrett. "Not just in terms of selling and buying, but also in terms of information transfer, education, and customer interaction."

Two short years ago Intel's Internet business didn't even exist. Yet in 2000 the Web generated revenues of $31 billion for the world's number-one microchip maker. The Web connection started modestly enough as a way for Intel's Asian customers and suppliers to place orders and get information more easily than by phone and fax. (The time difference between Asia and Intel's Texas headquarters didn't make it easy to transact business.)

According to Barrett, Intel's Asian partners were quick to adapt to the new system and processes. "We had people who went in to educate our customers: 'This is how we're going to communicate with you. These are the protocols.' And within a few months, some of these customers were suggesting improvements to our user interface!"

Today, more than 10,000 employees at 400 companies around the world, including Intel customers and suppliers, can order microchips, communicate with Intel engineers, and check on inventory levels. Even Intel customers and suppliers with electronic data interchange links to the company have switched to the Internet because it gives them more precise and timely information on inventory.

"Customers can now access information that's relevant to their company from anywhere and at any time," says Barrett. "In fact about a quarter of all transactions on our systems are done by customers after business hours."

Confidential information about Intel's new chips is now quickly distributed to design engineers at PC makers via the Internet. Passwords and security clearances ensure that this sensitive information is not leaked to competitors. Intel says that most PC designers believe the information reduces their development time by as much as three weeks—crucial in a business that has one of the fastest technology turnover rates of any industry.

In Asia alone, Intel's sales have grown 36 percent annually to $8 billion, and its list of customers has stretched to more than 170, up from 16 customers when the site was launched. "The Web has enabled us to take on more customers without growing head count," says Sandra Morris, Intel's director of e-business.

"Our customer service analysts now log 40 percent more orders in the same amount of time and spend 48 percent more time on high-value customer relationships than they did before the Internet," says Barrett. "And we reduced our order-error rate by 75 percent."

Internally, and also by reaching out to customers and suppliers, the Internet has transformed Intel's culture. "Everybody has to know what everybody else is doing," says Barrett. "Clearly, the Internet supports that philosophy by enabling rich, fast communication.

"We get technology," Barrett continues. "We make it, and we use it. We produce the basic building blocks for new technology and then wind up using those products almost instantaneously. We almost couldn't help becoming an Internet company."

Level 4

At Level 4 of participation, a company works to improve its own processes as well as and those of three other organizations, including its customers, suppliers, and partners. Once a company has reached this level of X-engineering, it's not unusual for its initiatives to change the processes of an entire industry. This is a natural result of successful X-engineering: Other players in an industry recognize that they, too, can benefit from process improvement and standardization. It will take courage, however, for companies to join in. They must see the benefits of shared efficiencies as well as the opportunity for their own true core competencies.

Companies participating at Level 4 come from industries as different as the office-supply and heavy-equipment manufacturing industries.

STAPLES

If any company defines the bricks-and-mortar business model, it's Staples, which pioneered the office-products superstore concept in 1986. Since then the company has grown to more than 1,300 locations in the United States, Canada, and Europe.

Unfortunately, Staples's e-commerce strategy hasn't been as prescient. Due to its own mistakes and miscalculations, Staples found itself playing catch-up to arch competitors OfficeMax and Office Depot, which launched online sales efforts in 1995.

Now Staples is making up for lost time by aggressively X-engineering on both the sell side and the buy side. The company is going full speed, conducting collaborative forecasting with its customers, partners, and suppliers; processing returns online; and even participating in standards bodies such as the Open Buying on the Internet (OBI) Consortium. In 1999 the company set the goal of one million online customers and $1 billion in online sales by 2001.

To meet this aggressive goal, Staples set up three discrete e-commerce businesses: StaplesLink.com for contract customers, Staples.com for small businesses, and Quill.com for customers with specialized needs, including medicine, law, and education. By the end of 2000, these combined businesses boasted one million users and more than $512 million in sales.

"The biggest strength Staples brings to the marketplace is its foundation in bricks and mortar and then adding the clicks to it," says Anne-Marie Keane, vice president of business-to-business e-commerce at Staples. "We had to look at this holistically. It's taken us years to develop the business experience in delivery, logistics, supply chain management, and customer care and to do it very cost effectively," she says. "You win the whole account, not just the electronic portion of the account."

Of course, Staples has made some missteps along the way. StaplesLink.com, designed to give corporate customers password access to contract pricing, proved cumbersome for customers to use.

"We found that many of our customers had never used a Web browser before," says Keane. "Or if they had, the technology was old and they hadn't upgraded."

Staples is addressing the buy side of the business, too. To better manage a supply chain with 400 to 500 vendors and more than 100,000 stock keeping units (SKUs), the company has installed stock replenishment software that automatically generates purchase orders for restocking and transmits them to vendors. Merchandise planning software lets Staples buyers collaborate with suppliers to match supply to customer demand.

In 1999 the company also established StaplesPartners.com to give its suppliers online access to information such as fill rate. "Right now, the site is a one-way street," says Dave Barclay, vice president of information systems for Staples. "Suppliers are able to get information off the site, including sales of their products for a given week by store or distribution facility, but we're not asking them to put any information onto the site." Soon, however, Staples will ask its supply partners to share data such as information on new products, which can then be filtered to Staples's Internet and extranet sites.

Anne-Marie Keane describes the Staples culture as "entrepreneurial," with a lot of projects going on simultaneously. The atmosphere at Staples.com blends office product sales vets with tech types skilled in e-commerce. To speed the collaborative process, all employees work on the same floor.

"Instead of waiting for answers to voicemail and e-mail messages, a developer can walk over to the business people and quickly hash out the best way to design a feature for customer use," says Keane. "A developer can make a design change in hours instead of days." As a result, development time has been compressed from 18 months to as little as 5 weeks.

In the end though, the final challenge for Staples is the biggest one of all: how to stand out in a business world built on commodities. Superior customer service, combined with innovative relationships with suppliers and partners, may provide the answer. But as you can see, Staples is experimenting with new processes to establish its distinctiveness. If an approach is successful and gets market traction, Staples builds on it. If an approach fails, it's abandoned. This is the continuous nature of X-engineering.

CATERPILLAR

Fortune 100 heavy-equipment maker Caterpillar is as big as the products it makes: More than 71,000 Caterpillar employees design, manufacture, market, and finance heavy construction, mining, and related equipment from more than 100 manufacturing locations around the world. Caterpillar uses more than 7,000 suppliers, and its revenue last year totaled over $20 billion.

With the broadest product line in the industry, Caterpillar believed it could drive costs down by linking its dealers and customers back through the supply chain in a build-to-order environment. In order to integrate the processes of its customers, dealers, and suppliers with its own, the company decided to develop an e-marketplace.

This marketplace is intended to transform Caterpillar's supply chain, logistics, planning, and customer management processes. When fully implemented, Caterpillar expects that it will shorten product introduction cycles, improve efficiency in design collaboration with suppliers, and reduce costs in ordering and fulfillment.

"A costly problem for any manufacturer with multiple locations is the duplication of parts that are essentially identical," says Mike Hackerson, director of e-business and business development for Caterpillar. "By recording parts design electronically, we have been able to drive out duplication from our inventory."

Caterpillar estimates that full rollout of its e-marketplace will take several years. So far, about 200 of its 7,000 suppliers are on board, and the company made its first sale of Internet-configured construction equipment in the summer of 2000.

"This worldwide initiative will support our suppliers, dealers, and customers and help us achieve cost and inventory reduction," says Caterpillar CEO Glen Barton. "Installation has begun, and benefits will be immediate. We anticipate a $100 million savings in the first year of operation." Barton expects that number to grow substantially in future years, making a major contribution toward Caterpillar's goal of reducing its cost base by more than $1 billion.

But Caterpillar is not stopping with its own business and those of its customers and suppliers. Caterpillar plans to work with i2 Technologies, Inc., to market the e-marketplace software to the heavy equipment industry and other manufacturing industries. "We're pleased . . . to make this unique software available more broadly," says Lynn McPheeters, Caterpillar vice president and chief financial officer. "The . . . Caterpillar solution has the potential to revolutionize the heavy equipment and engine industries as well as related manufacturing industries by improving interactions with suppliers." But the revolution will not happen just through software, it will happen as new processes are adopted industry-wide.

● ● ●

If well executed, X-engineering can, in fact, revolutionize industries. As companies move to Level 4 participation, industries will become dramatically more efficient, with effective, integrated networks of businesses and customers. But as the early examples in this chapter illustrate, the work begins at home with a more modest, but still challenging ambition: Get your own house in order.

Then, as you venture out to collaborate with partners, you must remember your manners. You won't be able to harmonize process across organizations unless you make yourself welcome. Here's some advice.

- Understand and respect the business goals of your partners. Like you, they are committed to their customers, and it is important to know what customer pull they are experiencing. You need to respect the strengths that they bring to an X-engineering relationship, as well as the business issues that they face.

- Be prepared to enter an active negotiation about the joint development of new business propositions and process redesign. Neither your ideas nor your processes may be the best. Don't be arrogant in the negotiations, especially if you are the largest company in the relationship.

- All partners should recognize the contributions of the process owners in their companies. The people who do this work need to know that they are appreciated.

- Maintain an open communications environment where you and your partners jointly assess your performance. Your judgment alone is not sufficient, and you may not be right.

- And finally, close the loop on all agreed actions. Every partner must do what it says it will do and be measured against the objectives to which it commits.

And how should you choose your partners? First, move cautiously. Although X-engineering calls for radical change, it is a continuous process, and you will live for a long time with your partners. Here are a few additional principles to help you avoid the disaster of flimsy alliances.

- Select partners who share your values. When you are jointly confronted with strategic, operating—and at times moral—issues, they won't be resolved unless you share a common or compatible set of beliefs and values. More on this in the next chapter.

- Find partners whose products, services, and territories are complementary—not in conflict—with yours. Once you have learned how to harmonize with this kind of partner, you may be ready to take on competitors as partners.

- Find partners who will create a changed and improved value proposition for your customers.

- Create combinations that will reduce the need for capital, not require more.

One partnership that has exhibited all these qualities is the Star Alliance, the combination of American and European airlines formed to create a virtual global travel network. Although the "alliance" word causes me worry, this combination has worked where other airline alliances have not. Why? Customers get to share frequent-flier air miles across airlines. The partners' geographic coverage is complementary, not overlapping. The partners also share information about customer travel preferences, so that they can create routes that respond to customer pull. And the combination has eliminated the need for some of the partici-

141

pating airlines to spend millions on redundant jets. There is something substantive in it for everyone.

But choosing the right partners does not alone assure successful X-engineering. X-engineering requires more than dealing with structure, strategy, and processes. It requires managers to change some of their behaviors, beyond just showing good manners. The next chapter moves into that topic: the managerial mind.

Chapter 9

What X-Engineering
Demands from You

Many executives spend much of their time pushing and pulling their managers through the minefields of technological change. They want them to be less anxious, more aggressive, and more imbued with "aspiration." But it is a tough sell.

What's required are equal doses of fear and desire, a guiding philosophy that reflects the ideas of Leonardo da Vinci. Though da Vinci is best known as the Renaissance artist who painted the Mona Lisa, he was also a super-polymath whose numerous inventions covered subjects as diversified as architecture and military engineering. His notebooks included drawings of what were to become the helicopter, the submarine, and the armored tank. In another notebook da Vinci analyzes his ambivalence about a dark cave. He writes that he felt afraid of going inside, yet eager to search for possible treasure. These twin emotions of fear and desire help move managers and companies as they adapt to the economic realities of today.

But, just as fear of the unknown can be beneficial because it spurs us to think clearly and to be more pragmatic, it can also paralyze an organization and prevent it from moving forward. Conversely, the desire to explore the unknown can motivate people to take chances that lead to wondrous discoveries. Too much boldness, however, can cause a company to ignore pragmatism and reality. A company can risk alienating its partners. It can exhaust its employees. It can disappoint its shareowners. How companies balance fear and desire will help determine their success today.

In balancing fear and desire as a means of motivation, I believe that company leaders should tilt toward desire. We have seen how organizations that rely primarily on fear—threats to the business as well as to personal growth and job security—have faltered. If companies are to realize the potential of X-engineering and meet the challenges it entails, their leaders will have to inspire through desire—with just enough fear in the mix to ensure healthy prudence and clear thinking.

Adapting to customer pull, for example, requires a depth of attentiveness and discipline with which many managers aren't familiar. Managers must be inspired to become increasingly intimate with their customers as they both search for and adopt new value propositions. And process push will extend many of the traditional concerns of management into the work, structure, and culture of other organizations, both suppliers and customers. Collaboration and influence will become more important than control.

Other shifts in managerial behavior will be required. Are managers prepared to expose their company's flaws? Will they openly share their ideas and processes? How will control, power, and authority be shared across organizations? Will a company's fundamental beliefs and values match those of its partners, and what will its managers do if there is a mismatch? These are just a few of the questions that X-engineering elicits.

In spite of these formidable challenges, the cycle of adapting processes to technology is going on apace. As dot-com skyrockets crashed and burned in 2000 and early 2001, major global companies, only recently derided as dinosaurs, were smoothly shifting their massive gears. In many cases, they directed their investments away from traditional information technology and toward Internet-based solutions as they recognized the importance that the Internet would play in the future of their business and the inevitability of X-engineering.

As former General Electric CEO John F. Welch, Jr., has acknowledged at an annual meeting in Richmond, Virginia, GE was initially slow to "digitize" its processes—the term Welch uses to describe GE's version of X-engineering. "We thought the creation and operation of Web sites was mysterious, Nobel Prize stuff, the province of the wild-eyed and purple-haired," Welch has noted. Then the global giants discovered that it was they, not the dot-com interlopers, that were best suited to play the new game.

"We have come to learn that digitizing all our . . . processes," Welch continued, "is the easiest part of the equation. We [already] have the hard part—hundreds of factories and warehouses, world-leading products and technology. We have a century-old brand identity and a reputation known and admired around the globe—all attributes that new e-business entrants are desperate to get."

Corporate managers have another major edge: experience with basic operating principles that need to be applied to new circumstances. Says Welch: "A technology change, massive as it is, doesn't mean abandoning traditional management concepts. What it does mean is adapting those business principles to the transforming of the world."

However, the adaptation Welch refers to challenges many of

the management tenets existing within companies. In this chapter I will discuss seven conventional precepts that must change.

The New Tenets of Management

OLD TENET: SEE THE WORLD AS YOU WANT IT TO BE.
NEW TENET: SEE THE WORLD AS IT TRULY IS.

A giant flying saucer from outer space is streaking toward Washington, D.C. It lands near the White House, where a welcoming committee of tanks and heavily armed soldiers awaits. A humanoid figure emerges from the saucer and explains his mission: to inform the world that placing hydrogen bombs in the hands of angry, fearful national leaders threatens the universe, including the alien's planet. Earthlings must allow themselves to be ruled by the same benign machines that govern his planet, thus preventing the possibility of nuclear war; the alternative is extinction. The visitor demonstrates his power by halting the operation of all earthbound mechanical and electrical devices. How will earth's leaders respond?

That was the question posed early in the 1951 science fiction film, *The Day the Earth Stood Still,* and it served as the lead-in to a message that Chuck Hora, the chief executive officer of the Lord Corporation, wanted to deliver to his managers.

Lord is a 75-year-old company with a sterling reputation as an innovator in adhesives, syntactic foams, and tape. Its scientists and engineers often work directly with customers in the design and development of products. In many ways, they are masters of upstream X-engineering.

But on this particular day, Hora wasn't sure that his managers were dealing realistically with the way information technology would affect their business. He pointed out to his audience that in the film, earth's leaders could choose how to respond. They could doubt the alien's identity; he might be a Russian agent. They could refuse to believe in his power. Or, confronted with proof of his power, they could look for a way around his ultimatum. As it turned out, the earth's leaders in the film were simply unwilling and unable to accept a new technological reality.

Hora wondered if his company's leaders, like their cinematic counterparts, were misinformed about and misguided in their reactions to the alien reality we live in today, specifically, the arrival of the Internet and its disruptive effects on commerce.

"I guarantee you, " he said, "that sitting in this room, are people who don't believe the Internet is here to stay, and others who know that it is, but continue to believe they have an alternative."

Hora is not alone in his plea to managers to face new technology and explore its eventual effects on their companies. Lawrence A. Bossidy, chairman of Honeywell, may have best pinpointed where X-engineering starts: "Effective leaders [have] a brutal understanding of reality."

Many managers, like many people in general, are made anxious by the prospect of change. So, despite the fact that the world is being transformed before their very eyes, in this case through technology, they don't alter their ideas or perspectives to accommodate the changes. They deny either the fact of the shifts or their significance. Indeed, they are out of sync with reality and, as a result, they are left behind.

Facing brutal reality requires facing technology's challenge as well as seeing the opportunities it creates. What should a manager do if, for example, he can see that, despite the large sum of money he spends on information technology, it has had relatively little effect on the efficiency or effectiveness of his business? Here is a little-known fact: 53 percent of all spending on equipment in the United States today involves information technology. Are managers getting what they need from this enormous expenditure? If they aren't, they are not alone. Estimates say that between 40 and

50 percent of major information-technology projects fail to deliver on their promises.

Here's another fact: 12 percent of all the capital stock in the U.S. is now invested in information and telecommunications technology—the same percentage that was invested in railroads at the peak of the Industrial Revolution, just before they collapsed. J. P. Morgan made his fortune by picking up the pieces. Who will pick up the pieces of the dot-coms and move forward?

Another brutal reality that must be confronted concerns the efficiency, or, more accurately, the inefficiency of industries. For example, right now, $600 billion of inventory is sitting in the supply chain of global high-tech industries. It does nothing every day except depreciate. Who's going to fix that?

Every manager must ask hard questions about her own company's performance. Where do customers' experiences break down? Are they loyal only because it costs too much to switch suppliers? What are the real costs of a company's processes?

Today, managers must be brutally honest when they measure performance. X-engineering begins with a fair assessment of where a company stands, and, more than ever, with the Internet making a company's performance increasingly visible, honesty must be the policy.

But if you are to see your company's role in the world as it truly is, you must also look to the positive side. What are your company's real strengths? What do your customers really expect—and receive—from you? Which of your processes are truly unique or proprietary? Once you know with confidence your real uniqueness—and you will probably be surprised at how narrowly that gets defined—you will be more prepared to let go of or share the rest.

OLD TENET: LEAVE INFORMATION TECHNOLOGY
TO THE TECHNOLOGISTS.

NEW TENET: INFORMATION TECHNOLOGY IS
EVERYONE'S JOB.

The Internet has made it abundantly clear that information technology is vital to business, and now managers must catch up.

Lord Corporation's Chuck Hora recently described the technology management skills that his company needs in unusual terms: "Even if I'm not a safecracker, if I sandpaper my fingertips, I can feel things better than if I don't. Even though I'm not going to be tumbling a dial and feeling the little balls falling into place, I will feel everything in my life more intensely if I sandpaper my fingertips. This is taking those rough edges, those cobwebs off our minds, making us more open to alternate possibilities and willing to embrace them when they come, because forewarned is forearmed."

As it stands, most managers don't have that kind of technology sensibility. They make large capital investments in information technology without half the knowledge or thought they would insist on if they were building a plant or production line. Technology awareness has become a core competency for everyone. Even in companies that outsource information-technology development and operations, managers must have a thorough, up-to-date knowledge of how information technology works in their industry.

I know managers aren't going to become information-technology experts, any more than they will know every wrinkle of tax law or antitrust policy. But just as they understand the impact of those rules on their strategy and operations, they have to become knowledgeable enough to understand how information technology will affect their business.

Of course, managers will still have to rely on technical experts for help with many technology decisions, just as they rely on lawyers and accountants. But, if they are not knowledgeable and comfortable with the world of information technology, they won't understand the experts' advice or take in its implications.

It is not enough to know how to navigate your company's e-mail and messaging systems or the latest wireless device. Though useful, those skills will not help in deciding whether investing $20 million in a supply chain management system is a good idea. Such decisions require hard-core knowledge and educated, soft-core intuition.

On the corporate side, managers need to make certain that their companies and partners accrue and maintain the technological expertise they require to compete effectively. Technology awareness has become a core competence. Even in companies that outsource information-technology development and operations, managers must maintain an up-to-date, robust knowledge of how information technology works in their industry.

Chapter 5 described the degree to which technology must be standardized so that a company's processes will operate in harmony with those of its partners. Managers must make sure that all of their partners are proficient with technology and have a technology infrastructure that will support X-engineering.

OLD TENET: INFORMATION IS POWER; KEEP GOOD IDEAS
INSIDE THE COMPANY.
NEW TENET: SHARE GOOD IDEAS WITH CUSTOMERS AND
PARTNERS AS YOU SEARCH NONSTOP FOR BETTER IDEAS.

Jack Welch pictures himself as a sort of maître d' of ideas. "My job is to listen to, search for, think of, and spread ideas, to expose people to good ideas," he once observed. "I'm getting the crowd to come sit at this table: 'Enjoy the food here. Try it. See if it tastes good.' And they do. When self-confident people see a good idea, they love it."

Such flexible receptivity to new ideas doesn't come easily to traditional companies, and GE learned it the hard way. In the 1970s and early 1980s, when many companies were involved in reengineering efforts, Welch realized that an organization's ultimate, sustainable competitive advantage derives from its capacity to learn, then to spread that knowledge throughout every part of the company, and, finally, to act on new information quickly.

With the aim of achieving that edge, GE broke down its internal boundaries, flattened its layers of management, and destroyed its organizational silos. It became standard procedure for GE people to share good ideas and perpetually search for better ones. As jealous hoarding of departmental ideas waned, so did hostility toward ideas from the outside. Welch purged the shibboleth of NIH—"not invented here"—from the system. The result, he says is "a company with an insatiable desire for information."

Technology has made that process easier for managers today. "Information is available everywhere, to everyone," Welch told shareholders at the company's annual meeting in 2000. In a sense, that availability makes opening up the corporate culture even more urgent and it also raises the price of failure. Welch concludes that "A company that isn't searching for the best idea, isn't open to ideas from anywhere, will find itself left behind, with its survival at stake."

X-engineering challenges companies to do more than spread good ideas internally. In a world where information flows freely, managers must contribute to the collective intellectual inventory of their customers, suppliers, and partners. None of them will want to pay for these ideas; they will simply expect them. Managers must be open both with their processes and their ideas.

There are direct benefits to being a generator of ideas. First, managers can improve their company's competitive positioning. Fidelity Investments, Inc., and The Charles Schwab Corporation are good examples of companies that are always pumping ideas into the financial-services industry, inviting anyone who can to copy them. Both companies have earned reputations as innovators in their industries and have mastered execution as well. There is significant competitive advantage in having your ideas and approaches become the standard in an industry. After all, you will have gotten there first.

The second advantage of generating ideas is that customers and partners will reward companies that help them solve their most confounding problems. Frequently, collaboration among the company, its partners, and its customers, especially when the company teaches the others everything it knows about a problem, can be the most effective approach to solving it.

OLD TENET: EXERCISE AUTHORITY TO GAIN CONTROL.
NEW TENET: GAIN CONTROL BY RELINQUISHING IT.

Traditional managers may be daunted by the prospect of managing in a networked environment—one in which they have no direct authority over many of the people delivering their goods and services. It is often hard enough to motivate your own employees to perform as you want them to, without taking on the employees of another company of which you are not the boss. A flat assertion of authority is not the answer. It simply doesn't work in a partnership. As a first step in a collaborative venture, managers must recognize that they are not in control, and that whatever authority they do have may come only by giving it up.

Before X-engineering, the idea that one could win control by relinquishing it was already being discussed. It was the subject of my book *Reengineering Management,* and it was espoused by a number of corporate executives. X-engineering revives this concept and places it at the center of a vastly different kind of management style.

X-engineered management pushes direct decision making down into an organization as well as out into other organizations. Since many of the people responsible for making decisions are more dispersed than they had been, it is imperative that managers and employees in every participating organization have easy access to all the information they require. Technology now makes it possible for that data to be delivered to the right person instantly.

Technology in general and the Internet in particular provide the framework for the power sharing that is vital to X-engineering. Along with facilitating globalization, deregulation, and the digital revolution, the Internet has sharply increased competitive pressures and transaction speeds. Leaders can no longer control decision making. They have neither the reach nor the time.

In today's complex, demanding business environment, leaders have no choice but to nurture and use the long-ignored ideas and experiences of frontline workers. Leadership is about setting guidelines and objectives and parameters, and then letting people go. It's up to the leaders to challenge minds, capture hearts, and allow others to make decisions and reach their full potential.

Among the top executives who subscribe to that view was GE's Welch. "I want to get to a point," he once said, "where people challenge their bosses every day: 'Why do you require me to do these wasteful things? Why don't you let me do the things you shouldn't be doing, so you can move on and create? That's the job of a leader—to create, not to control. Trust me to do my job, and don't make me waste all my time trying to deal with you on the control issue.' "

Leaders must also beware of the subtle seduction of power. "If you're the boss," Ron Heifetz, director of the Leadership Education Project at Harvard University, told *Fast Company*, "the people around you will invariably sit back and wait for you to speak. They will create a vacuum of silence, and you will feel a compelling need to fill it. You need to have a special discipline not to fill that vacuum." In other words, managers should control themselves, not others.

At Schwab, the old command-and-control leadership style has crumbled as the speed to market has soared. In the space of 15 months, the number of hits on the company's Web site skyrocketed from 6 million to 76 million. "We could not have handled that increase without the talent and creativity of every individual in the organization," says Schwab vice chairman Dawn Lepore. "At all levels of the organization, we need to solve problems, seize opportunities, and nurture creativity."

Lepore sees another way in which X-engineering has affected the relationships among executives and employees. It enables everyone to become a more demanding, knowledgeable consumer—feelings that carry over into the job.

Without question, X-engineering demands a level of teamwork that is rare in traditionally organized companies. To facilitate the freer flow of information that would keep all employees up to date and prepared to participate in decision making, leaders have to rethink their attitudes and behaviors toward those employees.

First, leaders should recognize that no individual can be well informed enough on such a plethora of issues to make all of a company's decisions. The leader's job is to set the larger goals, then make information accessible to everyone involved in executing it.

But, truth be told, maintaining the right kind of managerial control requires balance. Managers won't always be able to set goals, provide information, and sit back. From time to time, they will have to subtly or directly exert the authority that they have earned either from their position in the organization or from their particular expertise. Because the Internet will accelerate most management and operational processes, a business cannot always wait for an organization to make up its mind. Sometimes, telling people what to do is still the leader's most appropriate move.

Too often, for example, a successful, smart, and polite organization will procrastinate when making a final decision because its managers enjoy debating the issues and have lost track of the need to actually *make a decision*. They may have been given a false sense of security by the company's past successes. In such circumstances, a leader may have to "call the question" or make a unilateral decision. Such action should be the exception, though, not the rule.

Exerting authority cautiously but with effect requires knowing the territory, having a good sense of timing, and sensing how much force to apply. It is also notable that the word *authority* is closely related to the word *authentic*.

An important corollary to this tenet of control is that managers be authentic, that they do as they say, act as they prescribe. You can't do otherwise and exert the influence required in a transparent world.

OLD TENET: MANAGE CHANGE AS AN EVENT AND APPEAL TO INTELLECT.
NEW TENET: MANAGE CHANGE AS A CAMPAIGN AND APPEAL TO FEELINGS.

I learned early in my reengineering days that managing business change was not an event but a long journey. In fact, the metaphor of a journey fit reengineering perfectly. I recall how well one of my reengineering clients, Hallmark Cards, Inc., used that metaphor to inspire its people. (Hallmark is the Kansas City, Missouri–based greeting-card manufacturer that describes itself as being in the "personal expressions" business.)

As a way of launching Hallmark's reengineering efforts, the company's reengineering team and many of the people who would be affected by the proposed work changes were invited to a late-afternoon reception in the ballroom of a Kansas City hotel.

The team had already targeted the areas of process change intended to improve Hallmark's performance, and at the appointed hour, Robert Stark, the company chief executive officer, gave an inspiring and spirited talk in which he described the direction of the reengineering work and its expected benefits.

Hallmark's creative staff had constructed a large-scale model of a passenger steamship that filled one end of the ballroom. After Stark had given his talk, he walked up to the ship and broke a bottle of champagne across its bow. A live band embarked on a roaring marching tune, and the ship began to move slowly across the ballroom.

The symbolism was clear: The company had begun a long journey of change. My first thought was "corny!" My second thought was "brilliant!" What better way to appeal to people in a company whose business is about feelings and social expression?

But Hallmark did not stop with that event. Each month, the company issued a desk ornament that represented the journey. It signaled change in a joyful way. The journey was always repre-sented in positive terms, giving people more opportunity to create solutions to Hallmark's business challenges. In fact, there was no fear present. I recall meeting a member of the founding Hall fam-ily in an elevator one morning. His message to me: "You can do anything you want with this reengineering, but don't make our people unhappy." This company understood the importance of feelings in getting on with the journey.

The same sense of journey applies, of course, to X-engineering, but I cannot guarantee everyone happiness. A better metaphor for X-engineering may be a political campaign, one in which you must appeal to two populations: the intellectuals and the pop-ulists. Remember, X-engineering will involve work and business practice changes for thousands of people in many organizations. You may be able to convince a small number of managers within your own company and those of potential partner companies of the case for change—let's call this group the intellectuals. Your approach with this group will be to present the facts (the brutal reality I described earlier), set the business objectives, and achieve a balance of the partners' interests. If you are successful, you will have jointly negotiated the design of new processes and maybe even have won an argument or two. But of course you have only just begun; you have not yet improved business performance. That will happen only as work changes.

The challenge here is to understand the concerns and even prejudices of the people who will be doing the real work involved in the change. For example, when faced with the necessity to communicate primarily through electronic processes, they may argue that only face-to-face contact works with customers. Or they may feel that their work is a craft, requiring their personal and immediate attention and not susceptible to automation. All this requires that you be very public about what you are doing and sensitive to broadly held beliefs. You can change these beliefs over time, but that may not come until people have experienced the new ways of doing work. If your X-engineering is properly focused, they will eventually see both the need for and the benefits of the change.

OLD TENET: A MANAGER'S BELIEFS AND VALUES ARE HIS OR HER BUSINESS.

NEW TENET: A MANAGER'S BELIEFS AND VALUES ARE EVERYONE'S BUSINESS.

Until recently, if you wanted to speak with chief executives about their corporate cultures, they might have given you five minutes and a polite referral to the vice president of human resources. After all, CEOs dealt with the hard stuff (strategy, structure, and operations), and the human-resources people dealt with the soft stuff (people, behavior, and culture). But all that shifted in the 1990s when executives realized that the changes they were trying to bring about in their companies depended on their employees' skills and behaviors. In fact, there was no place more important for CEOs to focus their collective attention than on their companies' cultures.

As corporate metamorphoses became more the rule than the exception, managers searched for so-called transitional objects—that is, a facet of the company that was not changing that they could hold on to and bring from the "old" enterprise into the "new" one.

Clearly, the principles and beliefs upon which the organization was built would remain the same and should be carried over. Schwab's Dawn Lepore expressed it this way: "The velocity of change in today's economy requires a steady commitment to your fundamental values. We constantly tell our employees, 'Here's what's changing—and there's always something changing—and here's what isn't changing: Who we are and what we stand for.'"

In fact, Schwab's decision to X-engineer in the first place was rooted in its purpose and values. With the aid of the Internet, the company had the potential to provide what Lepore calls "the most useful and ethical financial services in the world," and actually enhance its image of ambition, fairness, capacity to earn trust, and teamwork.

In advising leaders of other companies, Lepore stresses the importance of "constantly communicating to your employees how and why your move . . . is consistent with your company vision. [Doing so] will go a long way towards ensuring your success." According to David Pottruck, Schwab's president and co-CEO, "If your goal is to build an important and enduring organization, you've got to spend a lot of time thinking about the culture that you're building inside your company."

A company's culture—its shared values and beliefs—develops internally for the most part. The fact that some companies promote, publish, proudly post, or market their values and beliefs does not diminish the genuine significance of their cultures to their purpose.

At the Bank of America Corporation in Charlotte, North Carolina, for example, the statement of purpose could not be more straightforward: "We help people realize their dream." Kenneth D. Lewis, Bank of America's chairman and chief executive officer, noted in a speech not long ago, "Whether that means owning a home, sending children to college, starting a business, or developing and strengthening a community, we are in business to make those dreams come true. Oh, we care about enhancing our profitability, too, but we do that because it helps us stay in business. In my opinion, anyone who doesn't understand this distinction shouldn't take on the responsibility that comes with a leadership position in business."

X-engineering demands that the company's beliefs and values be externalized even further. Of course, no one is suggesting that networked companies standardize or homogenize their cultural beliefs and values—such a move would hinder innovation and produce a boring and static business world. But ethics and behavioral standards must operate harmoniously across the linked organizations in the same way that processes do.

Simply put, managers must be sure that their company's beliefs and values will work well with those of their partners. Toward that end, here are a few questions to pose to potential X-engineering partners. Their answers will help you assess whether your cultures are compatible.

- What is the purpose of your business?

- How are its employees valued?

- How are customers regarded?

- How are technology and innovation experienced?

- Do you take quality and integrity seriously?

- How do you deal with breaches of trust?

- Are knowledge and intelligence valued and rewarded?

- Is change viewed as a burden or a benefit?

- Is there respect for the quality of operations and performance?

These questions will elicit the basic beliefs and attitudes of a company and its partners, which is precisely what they are intended to do. Confronting reality—a prerequisite for X-engineering—requires you to learn all you can about any company and its managers that you are considering as a partner. You must know what they really stand for.

OLD TENET: DON'T FIX IT IF IT AIN'T BROKE.
NEW TENET: RELISH CHANGE.

"It is not the strongest of the species that survive," wrote Charles Darwin, "nor the most intelligent, but the ones most responsive to change."

In the economic environment of the twenty-first century, where change is nearly continuous, Darwin's theory of survival applies to the world of business as well as it does to the world of biology. Undoubtedly, a company's capacity to respond quickly and adroitly to change will surely determine its long-term success or failure; hence managers must anticipate transitions, sometimes provoke them, and always embrace them with open arms.

Among the nation's largest companies, General Electric is noted for its rapid response to change. Jack Welch says that was possible only because the pace of acceleration was gradual. When the Japanese invaded some of GE's traditional businesses in the late 1970s and early 1980s, GE moved into different businesses and restructured its organization. It had a decade to adjust to that change.

When there were economic problems in Europe in the early 1990s, GE shopped for companies in which to invest; its window of opportunity that time was only two or three years. When it confronted similar dislocations in Asia in the late 1990s, the window was open for less than a year. "Today," Welch says, "the opportunities presented by change open and close on a weekly, even daily, basis." He believes that the gradual quickening of the pace taught GE's people to welcome change "for the competitive advantage it always brings and for the sheer excitement and fun it imparts to every aspect of business."

Yet, most companies have not developed GE's appetite for transformation. If everything is going well, managers are content to maintain the status quo. In fact, the most accepted mantra dealing with change in business today is "If it ain't broke, don't fix it." Such an approach precludes X-engineering.

In X-engineering, your aspirations are as important as your capacity for fixing broken processes. Managers who aspire to a higher level of business performance, who constantly search for new customer propositions, and who are committed to form new relationships that will help them attain their goals are well suited for X-engineering. These managers are also persistent, optimistic, and curious about what is to come. For them, change is relished, not dreaded.

But change does mean that work will be different, for managers as well as for the people around them. At Schwab, for example, many employees felt threatened when Web trading was introduced. "We talked with them about it," said Dawn Lepore. "We gave them Web access and asked them to help train customers—and they all aligned behind that goal."

This was a notable achievement. Technological changes, such

as the Internet, are more threatening to employees than other kinds of new initiatives. It can be daunting to be suddenly confronted with the need to learn a whole new set of skills. Anxiety and opposition escalate when the company actually moves ahead with X-engineering. And if all this comes on the heels of an earlier change program, people may feel understandably weary and cynical about the new proposal.

A good manager responds with a strong statement of the case for change and a heavy dose of inspiration. Eventually, when change is well executed, an appetite for it develops.

First, Last, and Always—Flawless Execution

Before we move on, I have one piece of management advice that is no less vital for being next to last: Execute flawlessly. When Bud Mathaisel, Solectron's chief information officer, was asked how Solectron was able to compete since it gives some of its "secrets" away, he said: "Our basis of competition is execution. We simply do very well what we say we will do."

Companies such as Solectron, EMC Corporation, Schwab, Wal-Mart Stores, GE, and Cisco Systems aren't secretive about what they are doing. Wal-Mart doesn't care who knows that it obsesses over its supply chain; GE's Jack Welch lectures publicly on how to manage. Cisco puts all of its processes on the Internet. What these companies have in common, beyond generating brilliant ideas, is the ability to execute nearly perfectly.

There is a long-standing academic debate on precisely this issue: Can a company compete on the basis of good execution? Eventually, some strategists argue, other companies will copy your ways, eliminating good execution as a sustainable competitive advantage. In reality, however, good execution is not easily replicated. The processes that work in one company do not necessarily transfer to another. Previous work habits and patterns of individual behavior can easily impede a company's ability to transform its way of doing business.

A competitor's arrogance may also work to your advantage. If its managers underestimate your ability to execute or it doesn't believe you're doing what you say, they will mistakenly pay you no attention. That hubris will eventually overtake even a very successful company by blinding it to what its competition is doing.

Of course, when execution starts to fail, the company's performance will degrade along with it, and these problems will be visible immediately to its customers and partners. That's the other side of transparency, the double-edged sword that the Internet brings to business. Managers must immediately detect the source of their problems. A business model may be flawed, as was the case with many dot-coms; operational processes may have been designed poorly or with too much complexity. Managers may be making decisions based on inaccurate information, or a company's electronic processes may not be adequately integrated with its physical processes. Wal-Mart suffered from all of these problems when it first established walmart.com.

Wal-Mart's first and fatal e-business flaw was its business model, which offered the entire range of its products—all 600,000 of them—electronically. Aside from the clutter, many of the items were not appropriate for online ordering and delivery. For example, one walmart.com executive keeps a 25-cent plastic cup in her office as a kind of negative talisman: The cup's two-day shipping cost was $8.

In addition to problems with its business model, walmart.com was unable to deliver goods properly; the execution failed because its systems were not adequately integrated with those of Fingerhut, its fulfillment supplier. Though it is expert at moving huge truckloads of goods into its stores, Wal-Mart had trouble dealing with single packages. Immediate delivery, usually a selling point for online shopping, was simply not possible.

Online customers were feeling the effects of the company's execution problems, which included receiving wrong information about their orders, particularly whether or not certain goods were in stock.

Wal-Mart recovered because it spotted the problems quickly and took aggressive steps to correct its initial mistakes. It removed many of the products that were inappropriate for online sales. In fact, it has found ways to use walmart.com to increase the efficiency of the bricks-and-mortar operation. One example: It now sells online the items that take up a disproportionate amount of space in its stores, such as patio furniture and appliances.

The Importance of Inspiration

In a recent conversation with a group of managers, someone said to me: "Five years ago we successfully reengineered our company. We dramatically improved our operations, and it allowed us to survive." But, he added passionately, "I'll never do that again. It was just too hard."

My first response was sympathy: I knew what he meant. When it is done well, reengineering is demanding, hard intellectual work. Jobs change, and some people cannot adapt. It always involves making tough decisions. This manager had done the work right; he just didn't want to do it again.

My second response was his company and others like it have no choice now but to take the next step, to X-engineer. Just as the competitive environment of the early 1990s required companies to radically rethink their operations, this decade's competitive environment and more demanding customers require companies to go further to eliminate inefficiencies, find new ways to compete, and form new relationships. This time, however, information technology will drive and enable the change more significantly. And with luck, having done all this once will make it easier the second time.

My third response was to wonder if there is a kinder, gentler way to X-engineer. If there is, it involves inspiration—and simply avoiding a number of common mistakes. That's the subject of the next chapter.

But, before we get to that, I should reemphasize the fact that a lot of people are tired. During the last 10 years, most companies have been reinvented, restructured, reengineered, and Six Sigma–ed; they have been downsized, upsized, and rightsized; they have searched soulfully for their mission, vision, and purpose; they have strategized and made hard choices. The work has gone on in corporate offices, seaside resorts, mountain retreats, and during long walks in the woods. In many organizations, multiple initiatives have been implemented simultaneously. People are confused.

At the same time that companies have been reinventing themselves, capital markets have become more demanding. Investors want both top-line and bottom-line growth, and the markets severely penalize companies that fail to produce them.

The dark side of information technology is also taking its toll on managers. Wireless communication devices intrude regularly on what had been private time, and technology seems to be accelerating all work processes. The urgent pushes out the important. There appear to be no boundaries between work and home. Some managers say they are breathless.

The answer is not to institute change as simply another program: Change, after all, is not a "program." It is a continuous, ongoing process, but in many companies it will require a fresh approach. You have now read enough to know that my approach is called X-engineering. You may call your approach whatever you wish. Just make sure that it has enough aspiration and inspiration.

Unfortunately, the decade has begun with a global economic slowdown and a new period of corporate downsizing. Nothing, of course, is slowing down in the process of technology-driven change. Yet, as always, the challenge contains opportunities.

Our goals must be to create new value for customers and to create a new workplace—a company without walls that connects with its customers and partners and facilitates work that, before now, was impossible. I'm describing the virtual company where people have access to all the information they need and knowledge is rewarded. And this, ultimately, is the cure for the fatigue and confusion that people may feel after decades of turbulent change. In this virtual company, all aspects of the workplace must be redesigned to counteract the weariness that employees and managers now experience.

Chapter 10

Ten Mistakes That
Every X-Engineer Should Avoid

In 1998 the Whirlpool Corporation, the venerable appliance manufacturer in Benton Harbor, Michigan, surveyed consumers on how they felt about buying dishwashers and microwaves. The study found that customers disliked shopping for appliances. They didn't know which machines were superior; they distrusted salespeople. *Consumer Reports* was helpful, they said, but its product reviews were often outdated. What they wanted was easy access to timely, reliable data that would enable them to compare brands and values.

In the fall of 1999 Whirlpool unveiled its shoppers' solution, a Web site called Brandwise.com. The site rated major brands as tested by the Good Housekeeping Institute. Visitors could actually buy the appliance of their choice online through an electronic link with the retailer of their choice. Even if a shopper bought a competing product, Whirlpool and Brandwise.com would benefit. The retailer would give the site 5 percent of the sales price on any Brandwise-enabled purchase. The site also expected income from selling consumer information to retailers and equipment test data to manufacturers.

Consultants and business journalists hailed Brandwise as a practical and pioneering venture. Eight months later, it was moribund.

The problems that bedeviled Brandwise included retailer resistance—many feared that the product reviews would favor Whirlpool, and they had no desire to pay the 5 percent fee. Many also lacked the advanced technology needed to keep real-time information flowing between retailers and the Web site. Worst of all, consumers stayed away from Brandwise in droves. With fewer than 200,000 visitors a month, the site was not even eligible to be followed by the Internet's traffic meister, Media Metrix. According to one theory about this fiasco, the planners overlooked the fact that most appliance buyers seek immediate replacement of worn-out appliances and have no interest in time-consuming research and slow delivery.

The Whirlpool story may seem out of keeping with this book. Up to now, I have concentrated on positive examples of corporate X-engineering because I believe that is the most effective way to illustrate my ideas. But I would be remiss if I overlooked failures.

In our personal lives, we often learn more from our mistakes than from our successes. Unless we suppress these things because they are too painful, most of us want to understand why something has failed. I know I can remember the details of every business error I ever made. Indeed, I can't forget.

So in this chapter my topic is mistakes, and how to avoid them. My major focus is on companies that tried to X-engineer themselves, but failed in the attempt. Some created special e-business units, launched major change programs, and spent millions to put technology infrastructures in place. In the end, they fell far short of the performance gains—major gains—that successful X-engineering provides. On top of all the waste in time and resources, the experience soured employees toward business improvement projects in general and their company's prospects in particular. Managers became ambivalent about the Internet's proper role in business.

What happened? Some unhappy managers blamed their mishaps on bad luck or bad timing. But X-engineering is more like chess than poker; victory is a function of knowledge, skill, and persistence. Luck is less important. If you know the rules and manage to keep yourself from making too many bad moves, you are likely to be successful.

In my study of X-engineering pitfalls, I found the same errors cropping up over and over. To help you avoid them, I have set forth the 10 most common mistakes below. Let's take them each in turn.

Mistake: You X-engineer before you reengineer.

One of the most visible examples of this error occurred in the Christmas shopping season of 1999. It was the heyday of Internet hype, and consumers responded accordingly. But retailers were taken by surprise when Christmas orders shot up beyond their expectations. Many were not operationally prepared to handle the increased volume. Many had poor fulfillment processes, and they certainly had not considered how to handle post-season returns.

Among the most visible victims were the Trappist monks. For years, Christmas had been the peak selling season for their fabled jams and jellies. In 1999 they planned to market their products even more aggressively over the Internet. Unfortunately, their planning did not go far enough in making sure they could fill the orders. The result was a lot of disappointed shoppers. But while the monks could be forgiven—they had a charitable purpose—consumers were harsh on e-tailers like Toys R Us, Inc., which irked thousands of parents with slow deliveries and out-of-stock items.

The hard lesson for retailers in 1999 was that X-engineering requires firm connections between your processes and those of your suppliers and customers. But if your processes are inefficient to begin with, their linkage across organizational boundaries is not likely to boost your company's performance. That's where reengineering comes in.

Let's assume that your corporation somehow escaped the wave of reengineering in the last decade. That means you are most likely still organized around departments and the individual tasks performed in those departments. The fragmentation and specialization that thrive in that environment can slow an organization to a crawl—hardly an advantage in today's fast-moving world.

Reengineering addressed that problem. It showed how a company could tear down the walls around departments and focus on the processes within and across them. It demanded the redesign of work from a process perspective. It worked, as many thousands of companies will attest.

But trying to impose X-engineering on a company that has not been reengineered is like putting a rocket on a Model T and assuming it will win the Indianapolis 500—or giving a B player a titanium racket and expecting him to win at Wimbledon. Companies need well-designed and efficient processes if they are to work more closely together.

Mistake: You X-engineer with executive commitment—but not involvement.

Sometimes it is hard to tell whether senior executives are really committed to a change program. I recall consulting to a large life insurance company whose executives had agreed to a new proposition: They would offer the best customer service in the industry. To back that up, they had unanimously agreed to spend $100 million to "reinvent" themselves. The reinvention would include designing new processes, developing new information-technology systems, building customer call centers, and extensive staff retraining.

A senior vice president was appointed to head the effort. And then one day a strange thing happened. His associates stopped coming to his meetings. They were ignoring the work, on which this company was spending several million dollars a month.

When I probed to find out what was happening, I discovered that all the executives had agreed to the conceptual idea of becoming the best in their industry for customer service, but they had never agreed on how to achieve that objective. Whatever commitment they had at the outset was now being abandoned in a silent campaign of non-participation. Their reaction was what I call the "ignore what's happening and this too shall pass" syndrome.

I learned from this and several similar experiences that to get people truly involved in an X-engineering effort, you must engage them early on. For one, you must invite them to talk out all the implications long before any process change begins. It is one of those times when you have to slow down in order to speed up later.

Whenever I speak to middle-management groups, the most common question is, "What do I do if my boss doesn't get it?" Some senior managers are so remote from the marketplace that they don't see the business case for change. Others support change in the abstract but fail to follow through. Still others are happy to lead the charge, but can't persuade their colleagues to join in.

Without senior management support, few major change programs ever succeed. The need for leadership from the top is even more acute in the case of X-engineering.

To X-engineer its processes effectively, a company must clarify its value proposition to its customers and its choice of corporate partners. These issues go right to the heart of the company's strategy. They must be discussed and resolved by senior managers; strategic decisions cannot be pushed down into the ranks.

In many cases, these decisions will require a company's executives to reinvest themselves in the details of a business. Making knowledgeable moves on an X-engineering chessboard requires a sophisticated understanding of customers and markets and of just how a company really operates.

I have also encountered senior managers who believe they can launch e-business initiatives and leave the execution to others. They abandon the budgeting process, for instance, to layers of management deep in the organization. Battles occur and compromises get made, but somehow enough funds are never invested where they are most needed, and the whole project goes nowhere. Your X-engineering program requires constant executive commitment and involvement; otherwise, it will surely fail.

Mistake: You confuse X-engineering with building a digital marketplace.

As the new century began, there was some promise that so-called "digital marketplaces" would provide the venue and the means for industry-wide X-engineering. In this book I have described many such marketplaces that have served as part of a company's X-engineering strategy. Some of them have succeeded, and some of them have now failed.

The theory was that these marketplaces would create standard processes—such as "request for proposal" and "order fulfillment"—that would operate across an industry and be used by all participants. These sites were first created as virtual trading floors for companies to buy and sell goods and services. The marketplaces would profit by taking a fee on each transaction. Some were developed by industry sponsors. Others were developed by buyer organizations. Covisint was formed by several major automobile manufacturers; Transsora was the work of major consumer-products companies.

Buy-side marketplaces have met with some success, but the industry-wide, sell-side versions have largely failed. There were simply too many of them—a dozen each in the metal and chemical industries alone. There was also the problem of transaction fees. Rather than paying these fees, buyers accessed the marketplaces simply to obtain information and then bought directly from the producing companies themselves.

I believe that one or two of these marketplaces will survive in each industry and that they will eventually develop standard processes to improve industry efficiency. But it will take some time before these processes are adopted broadly (I will discuss this later), and many marketplaces will run out of funding before they turn profitable. When the dot-com bubble gave them a potential value of billions of dollars, their sponsors were willing to put a few more million on the table to fund their development. But now, without the direct promise of big financial returns, investors and competing companies are less likely to support such efforts.

If your industry has a sound marketplace, you should participate. Otherwise, you will have to develop your own private marketplace, as General Electric has done with its "polymerland." A digital marketplace may, in fact, be a legitimate part of your X-engineering strategy. But remember, X-engineering is not just about doing electronic commerce. It is about adapting all your processes

173

to operate across organizational boundaries, and no one else is going to do that for you.

Just a year ago, companies not yet Internet-enabled were being chided with warnings like "It's not the big that eat the small, it's the fast that eat the slow." Nowadays, the slow are chiding the fast with boasts about the fortunes they saved by doing nothing. The new operative quip is "The second mouse gets the cheese." Don't believe that one, either. It is now critical both to understand and to get going with the changes that X-engineering requires. Even if there is an industry-wide marketplace that will provide you with some standard processes, there will still be lots of work to do in your company and with your partners. You cannot and should not wait to get on with it.

Mistake: You create a separate e-business.

For many companies, the logic of creating an e-business separate from the rest of the organization appeared to be undeniable. On the face of it, electronic commerce seems entirely different from traditional bricks-and-mortar operations, with their large office and sales staffs, their regimented work days, and their in-person connections with customers. The people who run and staff e-business operations tend to be an unconventional sort, and that was true of their initial online customers as well. The differences in business models and cultures argued for separate operations and even for launching a separate "new-corp."

In most cases, the e-prodigies that set out on their own with separate brands soon hit all the troubles of immature businesses. Independence further led some online operations to pursue business goals virtually at cross-purposes with those of their parent organizations, to the detriment of both. In some cases, new-corp units simply ran out of money.

It has also become apparent that many online customers are nervous about dealing with an entity that lacks a bricks-and-mortar presence, as though it might someday literally disappear into the ether. They want the option of dealing with a living, breathing person, a company with real assets.

All this argued for gradualism by organizations contemplating X-engineering, a point amply proved by online experimenters such as Bank of America Corporation, which is based in Charlotte, North Carolina, and ranks as the country's thirteenth largest corporation, serving 27 million households and 2 million businesses. According to Kenneth D. Lewis, the bank's chairman, president, and chief executive officer, some managers initially advocated a new stand-alone, electronic-only bank. In the end, the company simply added electronic banking to its financial services network of 4,500 U.S. offices, 38 international offices, and 13,000 automated teller machines (ATMs). Result: In 2000 the bank signed up more than 100,000 electronic customers a month; in 2001 the number exceeded 140,000 a month, for a total of more than 3 million online customers to date.

In the beginning, the bank's electronic customers were different from its overall customers, but that changed over time. I will let Lewis tell the story:

> At first, our online customers tended to stay with our company longer and to use more [products] than the average. However, as more and more customers joined us, it became increasingly clear that the early adopters represented a particular subset of our customers. Those on the leading edge tended to be customers who had a particular set of needs and characteristics, distinct from those of our customer base as a whole.
>
> But these days, online banking is being widely adopted by the whole range of our customers, and so we can no longer design the capabilities or plan the rollout with the early adopters in

mind. In fact, the bulk of the customers signing on and using the online channel tend to resemble more closely our general consumer population.

By avoiding the pitfalls of separatism, Bank of America has emerged with electronic banking designed to serve the needs of its total customer base. "Online banking shouldn't be a separate world, designed for a separate set of customers," Lewis has argued. "To the contrary, online banking brings increased choice, convenience, and functionality to all our customers, something we've been trying to provide all along."

Lewis's great insight was that almost all customers will eventually want to do some of their banking electronically. We can expect such transformations to appear first in industries such as banking that mainly provide customers with information. Sooner or later, the same customer pull will be felt in other industries.

Given the X-engineering principle that customer pull should determine how a company operates, it follows that eventually almost all of a company's processes will have to be X-engineered. A combination of customers' expectations and the benefits of X-engineering will demand a broad transformation. That cannot happen in a company that relegates its e-business activities to a separate unit or just launches a new-corp as its entry to the digital age. In those cases, the learning and transformation of the new units never reach into the main part of the business, where most of a company's profits are usually made and where change must occur in order to preserve those profits.

Back in 1999 Jack Welch became aware of the Internet's importance. He commanded his troops at GE to undertake a broad transformation program comparable to what I now call X-engineering.

At first, a number of GE divisions established independent e-business units, but that proved to be temporary. The majority have now been brought back into the company's mainstream businesses, where they can better serve the overall goals of the parent company. "The Internet," Welch told *Forbes* recently, "is all about growyourbusiness.com, not destruction. In the end, it's everyone's job."

Mistake: You move too slowly or too quickly.

Successful X-engineering requires knowing how to adjust your rate of change to the readiness of your markets and the capabilities of your company and your partners. You need to know when to move quickly and when to slow down.

Speed isn't just about getting to market at any cost and building market share, as Internet hype would have you believe. Speed is about moving at the right pace to keep X-engineering momentum going while not wearing people out in a forced march. But "organizational artifacts" can conspire to slow you down, so much so that your X-engineering effort could crawl to a halt.

Recently I tried to help launch an X-engineering effort in a large hospital system. The chief executive, a brilliant health care visionary, was committed to improving the experience of the hospital's patients. To accomplish this, he would have to change many processes and connect with many other service providers. His vision was similar to that of Charlie Baker of Harvard Pilgrim, which is described in Chapter 1.

But the hospital system's medical staff resisted the required changes. They saw a threat to proper medical practice as they defined it. Some of their concerns were well founded, others not, but the debate dragged on so long that little energy was left to move forward with any real changes. Eventually, the CEO received an offer to head another hospital system, and he took the job—hoping to be more successful there. After he left, the X-engineering effort just petered out.

When Jack Welch was once asked to look back over his years with GE and identify his single worst error, his response was surprising. "My biggest mistake was agonizing too long over difficult decisions," he said, adding: "GE would be better off if I had acted faster."

As much as anyone, Welch was early in recognizing that business today proceeds at a pace beyond the imaginings of a decade ago. Yet even he has had trouble keeping up. Stephen M. Case, chairman of AOL Time Warner, Inc., described the change in these terms: "You know the song 'What a Difference a Day Makes'? Well, in our business, the song we sing is more like, 'What a Difference a Nanosecond Makes.' "

Case referred to more than the phenomenal speed of today's technology. He was talking about the speed required of the people who lead and operate today's organizations.

Many managers still prefer to operate at a deliberate pace. They were raised to believe that the best decisions emerge from exhaustive pow-wows. "Make haste slowly" is their motto. My own experience suggests that the smarter the people in an organization are—think engineering cultures and hospitals, research and development departments—the more they are inclined to indulge in seemingly endless debate. Too often the issue is talked to death, and no action is taken.

The danger is greatest in the world of technology, where a fondness for discussion and delay can easily derail change. Schwab's Dawn Lepore echoes that warning. "If your company does not have a history of . . . moving quickly," she says, "your transition to the Internet will be more difficult."

This is not to suggest that you leap on the first proposal that appears and gallop off into the technology future without exploring the trail ahead. Not everything in business should move at Internet speed. Even if you can X-engineer your company to change and adapt quickly, for example, your customers and suppliers are unlikely to move quite as fast. You must allow them a reasonable adoption time.

Within your own organization, though, once you make your basic X-engineering decisions, you must move forward, committed to a course until some clear market signal suggests that you should change your approach or moderate your speed.

In the end, almost every business process—and almost everything else in your world—will experience a time compression because of the Internet. The effect will not always be comforting. Many managers I meet today seem breathless or worn down by the intensified speed of their work lives. They can expect more of same. There are no predictions that the rate of change is going to decline.

Begin to adapt by being more discerning in the way you allot your time between work that is important and work that is not. Dump the unnecessary stuff. Your exhaustion may come more from foolish work than from the speed of change. And, from time to time, take a break from your routine to restore your equilibrium. You need to maintain a balanced point of view.

In a sense, I am suggesting that you occasionally slow down in order to improve the way you're speeding up. The net effect should be better X-engineering that goes faster than you once thought possible.

But remember: Going slow and taking too long can also wear people down. Speed in X-engineering is about knowing when to go slow and when to accelerate.

Mistake: You start by focusing on units that aren't open to change.

For most companies, there will be no shortage of processes that would make ideal candidates for X-engineering. Where should you begin?

Clearly, it should be in whatever unit you consider most receptive to accepting the new ways of doing business with enthusiasm and intelligence. You want your first efforts to send a powerful message to the rest of the enterprise: "See how work can be transformed, how business performance and personal lives can be improved. X-engineering can do the same for you."

The optimum starting point is not necessarily so obvious. You might assume that the people who stand to gain the most from cross-organizational linkages would be a logical choice, or that you should begin with those who are already most knowledgeable about the benefits of technology. In fact, depending on the nature of the company and the behaviors involved, those two groups might well be the worst of all possible pioneers.

Cisco Systems was well on the way to a major mistake in the early 1990s when John T. Chambers, now chief executive officer, persuaded the board to begin investing heavily in information technology. Cisco had previously spent only 0.5 percent of its revenues on information technology. Chambers argued that X-engineering would vastly improve customer service—and therein lay the looming pitfall.

Since customers were his main focus, the obvious place for Chambers to bet on was the customer-wise sales department. The second best choice seemed to be engineering, since the engineers were techno-literate. But Chambers also observed that those two units were "my most independent and headstrong groups." Even if they welcomed X-engineering (and bigger budgets), they were quite capable of running away with the experiment and confusing or even destroying it in the process.

Chambers thus realized that the most likely change agents were also the least likely to achieve success, a paradox we should all consider. This was true at Cisco; it might well be the opposite at your company. When it comes to changing a corporate culture, those in charge had best remember the old saying that "all politics is local."

In the end, Chambers shrewdly went with the units in charge of order fulfillment, finance, and manufacturing. And their positive experience paved the way for X-engineering the company as a whole. As I mentioned in Chapter 5, 87 percent of Cisco sales today are handled on the Cisco Connection Online. It also takes care of 4 million requests for information a year, which saves Cisco about $250 million annually.

Instead of overwhelming success, John Chambers might have encountered overwhelming failure had he started his program with sales and engineering. These are some of the factors to consider in choosing where to start X-engineering: A business unit's appetite for change; the size of the business opportunity; the local culture. Wherever you start, keep this in mind: A company can manage only a limited number of change initiatives at one time.

Mistake: You X-engineer only the front-end of your business.

The dot-com graveyard is littered with companies whose business change consisted of creating a Web front-end to their current business. Some of these ventures were launched by bricks-and-mortar companies; others were well-funded start-ups. But they had this in common: a failure to link their customers to their organization's logistics processes. As the highly visible delivery and service breakdowns during the holiday season of 1999 made clear, doing business over the Internet requires much more than a new customer interface.

Over the past decade many managers have spent vast sums on information technology, both to prepare for the year 2000 and to redo enterprise-wide systems. Now they can hardly believe how little they got for their money in terms of improved business performance. The hard truth is that they did not go far enough in process change.

But it also may not be enough just to smoothly link your electronic sales channels to your logistics processes. As we saw in the case of W. W. Grainger, and its partners (Chapter 5), there is a lot to rethink, including how you define and catalog products—and even the very nature of your product or service. That's part of your proposition work.

Remember my earlier story of the life insurance company that aspired to lead its industry in customer service? After spending lavishly to reengineer its customer service processes, the company discovered that its products were too complicated for customers to understand. Any increase in service simply worsened the problem. The only solution was to go back to square one and greatly simplify the company's products.

The U.S. Internal Revenue Service (IRS) has a similar problem. It has recently become widely known that only 65 percent of the service calls made to the IRS are answered. There simply aren't enough service operators available to respond to all taxpayer queries. The agency could hire more help or automate the inquiry and tax filing processes, but neither fix would work. First, the IRS needs to simplify the tax code that generates all the needless complexity. At last count, the agency was grinding out enough paper each year to wrap around the earth 28 times. Doing that electronically may save some trees, but it adds little value.

And if you limit your change work to front-end processes, you are going to miss crucial opportunities to harmonize your upstream processes with customers and suppliers.

Mistake: You X-engineer all your processes at once.

X-engineering demands a total rethinking of your processes, but you can't implement everything at once. You do, after all, need to maintain your company's manageability, and you also must retain a consistent presence in the market.

If you have experience installing enterprise-wide systems, you will know what I mean about manageability. These are the systems that perform most of a company's business functions, from human resource management to finance to customer service to order fulfillment. The first mistake that companies often make is to buy a large suite of software before they have considered the scope and design of their X-engineering efforts. They assume that, magically, new systems and processes can be simply dropped into the company. The predictable result: disaster.

I thought that most companies had learned their lessons in earlier reengineering days, but many are making even bigger mistakes as their need and ambition to change have increased. Recently, I found one company that had been involved in an enterprise-wide systems and process effort that had taken five years and cost $80 million; the new processes are still not operating.

The problem was that the company's executives saw the change as being principally about technology and gave little or no attention to their processes and business execution. X-engineering is technology-enabled, but that does not mean it should be left to a company's technology staff to manage. Nor does it mean that you can rely on outside software services and products to accomplish your business change. This combination of naïveté and hubris must be replaced by a thorough consideration of how processes work and by a careful orchestration of process change, timed to the needs and managerial abilities of the particular organization.

But even when a company pays scrupulous attention to the manageability of change, its ambition to introduce new services and products may well exceed the market's ability to absorb these offerings. In dealing with X-engineering services and products, remember that you have to change not only your processes, but those of your customers and suppliers as well. That doesn't happen overnight.

Mistake: You believe that e-business is about the e.

Whenever I attend a conference on e-business or the Internet, I am struck by the emphasis on technology and the lack of attention to how business really gets done. This over-focus on technology and lack of well-developed business thinking was behind many a dot-com failure.

Yet even today many proponents of technology-driven business change maintain their over-infatuation with technology. Recently I attended a health care conference dedicated to the changes the Internet would bring to that industry. Extensive global studies were presented on the industry's readiness for change—a country-by-country report of laptop and wireless penetration; the number of Internet service providers operating in each country; the degree to which doctors and hospitals were wired. For conference participants, "readiness" was defined as the extent of a country's information-technology infrastructure. No one paid any attention, for example, to how "ready" doctors were for process change.

Most doctors I know are, in fact, eager for process change. In the United States, for example, they want processes that will improve their interactions with managed care, which they experience as controlling too much and paying too little. In less developed countries, doctors are keen to gain access to information about treatments and outcomes. They have no desire for electronically enabled processes that will reduce the time they can spend with patients.

In my research for this book, I had the opportunity to observe doctors using new patient information systems. The systems were designed to capture clinical data during a patient's examination. The doctor was required to turn to a computer terminal and enter data into a clumsy system before he or she could close out an examination and release the patient. The doctor experienced all of this as a distraction and as detrimental to his or her patient relationship. That happens all too often in medicine and elsewhere when systems are designed with too much attention to the *e* for electronics and not enough attention to the *p* for process. It goes back to a point made early in this book: Businesses need to intelligently apply technology.

Mistake: You underestimate adoption time.

Don't expect your customers to accept X-engineering at anything like the speed you do. Overnight customer conversions almost never happen. In most cases, you will be preaching to the unconverted considerably longer than you might have hoped. Even so, you must stay in tune with your customer base. That means staying only slightly ahead of your customers; it also means retaining their option to do business the old way. Remember that perhaps 90 percent of your customers are accustomed to pre-electronic processes and may well feel pulled to stick with the familiar rather than pushed to explore the unknown.

At the same time, you cannot drift along waiting for your customers to encounter some revelation—some e-piphany, if you will. To stay competitive, your reengineering and X-engineering programs must go forward while you gradually introduce your customers to the new ideas and they gradually get used to them. Ideally, you will both arrive at the starting gate at the same time.

This is a two-track process, and one way to manage it effectively is to launch your company changes on the premise that customer adoption will occur early but that you will be prepared for the possibility that it will be late. In other words, keep your traditional processes thriving in tandem with your X-engineering efforts. This puts you in a prime position: while 10 percent of your customers happily accept X-engineering without hesitation, you are set to serve the laggard 90 percent whenever they begin slipping into the fold piecemeal. Whether total adoption takes one year or five, you can serve both worlds and your business continues unabated throughout.

Many companies, for example, use a multiprocess approach to order entry. They tell their customers that they can order products or services by telephone or fax, or over the Internet. In time, they offer customers incentives to move to the Internet, usually the low-cost alternative for both a company and its customers. Eventually, customers experience the benefits and make the shift. But this strategy requires time, money, and persistence.

The early e-business environment was inspired by a famously failed maxim: If you build it, customers will come. Guess what: They didn't come fast enough or spend enough, and too few came at all. The business models of most e-business start-ups and digital extensions of bricks-and-mortar businesses assumed a high speed of customer acquisition and fast growth. When that didn't happen, most of them ran out of money.

Another common mistake was the assumption that advertising would accelerate growth. Many new business-to-consumer ventures—and, to a lesser extent, business-to-business ventures—spent enormous sums on advertising to attract customers. They simply ran out of money faster than the others.

Remember, real X-engineering is not just about selling products or services. It is about convincing your partners and customers to join in process change. It requires active negotiation to change the way work gets done beyond your gates. For example, if you are going to invoice electronically, customers will have to learn—and want to learn—to pay electronically. You must convince them that there is a significant business case for a change: A paper invoice takes on average $15 to produce and deliver, an electronic invoice only 25 cents.

True, the world isn't rushing to do business this way. It will take time—measured in years, not months—as well as collaboration and education before the full work process change takes place.

To speed it along, be sure you choose the initial process change areas carefully. Where will customers and partners quickly see X-engineering's benefits? Also be sure that you have a financial model for your business that will bankroll your operations until new processes are adopted and business performance starts to take off. Don't spend too much too fast and remember that patience and persistence are essential.

Don't focus on defense.

And while you are busy being careful not to make any of these ten mistakes, don't focus on defense. Today the term "protected markets" is an oxymoron—no company's market is safe from technically advanced upstarts, ambitious suppliers, or invaders based in other industries.

There is no point in hunkering down in a corporate bomb

shelter, spending days devising new ways to hold on to what you have. The ways in which competitors can take it away are so many, and so unpredictable, that a defensive stance is simply no longer practical. You need to attack your weaknesses, attack your markets, attack the future.

I cannot help but think of Xerox Corporation, that once powerful company with the wonderful new product that swept all before it for so many years. But Xerox was so busy defending itself and its product and its market share that it failed to see that the new forms of information transfer were inevitably going to take over the lion's share of its business.

Instead of taking the lead in ushering its customers into the paperless era, instead of moving with the times from a focus on documents to a focus on information, Xerox sought to defend its status quo. It was the wrong way to go.

It still is. "Those with something to defend must be flexible and opportunistic," says James H. Hance, Jr., vice chairman and chief financial officer of Bank of America, "or they will probably lose what they are defending anyway."

To be sure, you cannot ignore your everyday responsibility for fending off challenges and maintaining profitability with your current products and services. But your stance, your mental state, should be proactive and attack-oriented.

And that holds for all of your processes and systems. Adapting your company to the reality of a technology-based economy should not be simply a defensive move, as in, "Everybody's doing it." Nor should it be a minimalist move: "See how little we can get away with." If you are not ready to attack, to break new ground, to redesign the basic processes of your organization to make the most of this potent new technology, X-engineering is not for you.

Chapter 11

X-Engineering in Action—SciQuest

The examples that I have used in this book to illustrate X-engineering—with the exception of Cisco Systems, Dell Computer Corporation, and eBay—have been companies that began with a traditional structure and a set of common business processes. In one way or another, they have all worked to reinvent themselves. I have selected these "traditional" companies that are doing extraordinary things because my purpose here is to advise the leaders and managers of just such organizations on how to accomplish corporate change at a time when technology allows a whole new way of operating.

You will also notice that up to now I have not written much about the dot-coms, that class of company that was developed principally to do business over the Internet. They continue to fall by the wayside as I write this book. What distinguishes them as a group, their troubles aside, is the fact that most of them are not complete businesses. They simply lack the processes and capabilities to succeed. Their incompleteness derives from the short-term perspective of their investors and the naive assumption of their managers that they could buy any capability that they could not build. They are not good examples of what I mean by X-engineering.

There is one dot-com company, however, that does serve as a complete case for what X-engineering can be. Frankly, I like this company. Its managers have the right ambition and the intelligence to succeed. And although the company has been challenged by the current economy and by Wall Street's skepticism, I want you to consider what it has accomplished and how, over a relatively short period of time, it has changed its proposition to respond to the pull of customers. It is a great example of corporate learning and nimbleness.

The Story

There was a time when Scott Andrews was having a lot more fun. Think back to when the cofounder and chief executive officer of SciQuest.com was toasting the new millennium. His company, which was then offering a buying service for scientific supplies, was flying high; its initial public offering had quintupled from its $16 debut, ending 1999 at $84.13. And Andrews was a hero to his friends and family in little Farmville, Virginia, who had invested $125,000 in SciQuest back in 1997 and had seen their stake mushroom to $17 million.

Less than a year later, Wall Street's dot-com euphoria had vanished. SciQuest had laid off 10 percent of its 415 workers, and the stock was languishing at $2.50. But Andrews was stubbornly unbowed. Wall Street was just spooked, he said, and had never really understood the SciQuest story. SciQuest had $90 million in the bank, more than 1,000 regular customers and a list of 750 suppliers, and at least some investors who still believed in the concept of making it easy and efficient to buy scientific equipment and supplies. "I don't think they are just whistling in the dark," analyst Robert Fontana of Wachovia Securities told reporters. "At the end of the day, their customers need what they supply."

Indeed they do. It would be hard to imagine a task more fragmented and complex than the one confronting a scientist trying to buy laboratory tools and supplies. There are 2 national distributors of lab materials and perhaps 50 regional distributors, all of them dealing mainly in standard supplies—test tubes, Bunsen burners, centrifuges, and common chemical and biological compounds. But, in addition, there are perhaps 3,500 manufacturers and small suppliers who sell sophisticated specialty goods and are not represented by the distributors. Together, the small suppliers account for two-thirds of a global market estimated at $36 billion. For questing scientists, that spells a logistical nightmare: poring for hours through literally hundreds of catalogs to find the precise gadgets or compounds they need, and then having to deal with the paperwork for dozens of suppliers.

In short, it is a business that cries out for X-engineering—and Andrews, now 35, came to that conclusion some years ago when he was a salesman for Baxter International, Inc., one of the industry's major suppliers. He and a fellow salesman, Bobby Feigler, sketched the idea for SciQuest on the proverbial paper napkin in a sandwich shop in Durham, North Carolina, and started the company with two of Andrews's schoolboy friends from Farmville, Peyton Anderson and Keith Gunter. Today it has evolved into a technology company that enables researchers and laboratories to shop for nearly 2 million products from 800 individual suppliers. In fact, SciQuest is a new class of company—one that has leveraged the Internet to offer the systems, information, and process knowledge that make it possible for customers to X-engineer themselves.

None of this came easy. The four founders quit their jobs, liquidated their 401(k) plans, borrowed on their houses, maxed out their credit cards, and went without paychecks for 21 months to get their idea up and running. Collectively, they were in debt for nearly $500,000 before turning the corner. But then they found $700,000 in "angel money" from a group of high-net-worth individuals, including the $125,000 from friends and family in Farmville, and eventually raised $50 million in capital before their IPO brought in another $128 million in November 1999.

Even with money in hand, SciQuest wasn't an easy sell. The scientific community was slow to realize that the network was there, and even slower to start using it. As Andrews recalls it, there were no more than 10 customers in the company's first two years. Meanwhile, the online catalog had to achieve the critical mass that would attract customers, and that was slow and difficult. It had to provide easy, logical access to thousands of products, each of them with dozens of variable features, and it had to be infinitely expandable as new suppliers signed up.

In the beginning, the catalog was just an interactive directory: Buyers could find what they wanted in it and then e-mail orders to the individual manufacturers. SciQuest was to get its revenues from advertising. But when such revenues proved elusive, the company changed its business model. For a period of time, suppliers paid commissions on what SciQuest sold. They were charged rates that varied with the complexity of the product, the strength of the supplier's brand, and the costs of handling transactions. Today, SciQuest is paid a license fee by buyers and suppliers for access to the company's technology and services.

In the pages that follow, we discuss SciQuest's evolution in X-engineering terms, focusing on its processes, proposition, and participation.

Process

Process knowledge is SciQuest's core capability. It sits at the heart of the company's ability to manage the scientific supply chain for its customers, both as to its search processes and its customer-relationship processes. "We really pride ourselves on the experience that we deliver for our customers," Andrews told me.

In practice, he maintained, there are two main varieties of the scientific buying experience. Most commonly, scientists know what they need and where to find it, and SciQuest's role is to allow them to get it quickly and easily on the Web. That's an edge Andrews means to keep. But the other kind of transaction is even more important to SciQuest—the 40 percent involving buyers who don't know exactly what they need or who makes it. The truly hard part is building an electronic catalog that will give them a superior shopping experience, finding the answer and placing the order with two or three clicks of a mouse. That, said Andrews, "is very complicated." Every different product category has many variables. Antibodies, for example, have 42 attributes. "How in the world do you set the search methodology and the comparison tool to deal with antibodies and, say, distillation flasks in the same order?" Andrews demands.

But that is just what SciQuest has painfully learned: how to attack a new product category, ask the right questions of consumers, and deliver a satisfactory experience. And that expertise must also remain proprietary, Andrews said, "because quite frankly, we think that's the company. That is where we completely build a niche in our market space."

The SciQuest selling process is another unique competency. "Our customer relationships are critical," Andrews explained. "It's been a huge competitive edge for us to manage customers' expectations, to understand their needs so we can build the right products." And the cutting edge of this process comes in customizing the sale for each customer. For most buyers, Andrews noted, "our core solution addresses perhaps 80 percent of their needs, but it's that last 15 or 20 percent that we configure specifically for each customer that gives us our competitive advantage. We have had to build that competency internally. No other vendor's solution could customize it as well as we do."

Andrews recognizes, however, that not all processes must be proprietary, and he is willing to share some. Basic content management of the e-catalog, he told me, might well have been outsourced if that competency had existed when SciQuest was founded. Since it didn't, SciQuest's people had to develop it on their own. Now, having done so, he said, "We are hoping that some of the other companies in our industry will outsource us."

SciQuest recently established a new offering, Content Services, with an eye to sharing some of its proprietary processes with outsiders. Content Services will explore the possibility of managing its suppliers' catalogs and Web sites just as it does its own, charging a fee for the service. Eventually, SciQuest might even manage content for its competitors' catalogs. Sometimes, a small piece of a big pie is worth more than a big piece of a small pie.

But one problem that Andrews has not solved is the lack of standardized information systems. As I described in Chapter 5, this problem is systemic in all industries and must be addressed to fully leverage the Internet. Andrews explained that laboratory suppliers use 30 to 40 different technologies for managing finances, inventory, and orders, and each system may have five variations. Major companies tend to be committed to sophisticated EDI systems, while some mom-and-pop suppliers still handle orders with fax systems. SciQuest is pushing for standard formats for catalog listings, order transmission and acknowledgment, and order forms.

"We're taking EDI and putting it on steroids, to make it a little more flexible and robust," Andrews said.

Proposition

SciQuest began basically as an online supplier directory for its customers, permitting them to contact suppliers after the customers determined their needs. In its second generation SciQuest became a total buying solution, giving buyers a wide range of options, from "cradle to grave" sourcing to disposal.

Suppliers paid SciQuest a commission on every item sold through its service. But like many companies that sought to leverage the Internet to help buyers navigate through fragmented markets, SciQuest found that it could not sustain its new business model. It was providing a valuable proposition to both its customers and suppliers, but suppliers eventually balked at paying commissions.

Undaunted, Andrews and his team took their technology capability, extensive process knowledge, and wealth of catalog information and began offering these as a service to the buyers of laboratory supplies. With SciQuest's help, buyers can now build these search and acquisition processes right into their own organizations.

A customer begins by logging onto SciQuest.com and going to the company's private marketplace, a searchable online catalog that permits browsing by product or supplier and lets the buyer place a direct order to any of company's suppliers.

Customers can explore such specialized areas as the Chromatography Column Shopper, the Antibody Shopper, and the Bio-Supplynet guide. They can click on SciCentral, an online source of scientific news and research that is updated daily.

To buy an item in the private marketplace, a customer compares products and prices, decides on a purchase, and clicks the mouse. SciQuest's SciConnect feature seamlessly meshes the buying procedure with the customer's own corporate procurement system, while the EasyApproval service works within the buyer's organization to get all the necessary requisition approvals. The entire purchase can be accomplished with a single mouse click.

SciQuest goes to considerable lengths to make dealing easy for the suppliers listed in its electronic catalog, as well as its customers. Catalog data can be transferred from practically any electronic system, or even loaded from a printed source; then it can be scrubbed and massaged to enhance its appearance and updated electronically as needed.

All told, said Scott Andrews, SciQuest is positioned to provide buyers with a unique electronic buying experience.

Participation

Although SciQuest's proposition now is to help its customers X-engineer their own processes, along the way it learned lots about participation. Getting hundreds of suppliers and thousands of customers to buy into SciQuest's original proposition was no mean feat. By the same token, it was no walk in the park for SciQuest to get suppliers to standardize processes and information systems, while it was harmonizing buying and selling processes with its customers. SciQuest was initially able to accomplish this because it recognized that it really had two kinds of customers: end users—scientists who need equipment and supplies and want an efficient and effective buying experience—and suppliers. So the company developed a series of strategic propositions to offer both sets of customers. The essential element in those propositions, Andrews noted, was the assurance that SciQuest could be trusted to be a neutral marketplace.

Historically, the national and regional distributors who have dominated the scientific equipment market have concentrated on the commodity side, selling standard supplies in bulk. That alone gives SciQuest market opportunity, according to Andrews: "We are going to solve more of the customers' challenges than anyone, because we are dealing with about two-thirds of the critical research products, not just commodity items."

Trust is also a factor. The big distributors tend to favor major manufacturers and products on which they can make the most money. SciQuest remains "supplier neutral" and this is valued by some buyers.

The two national distributors are gearing up to offer electronic purchasing, Andrews said, but "we don't see them as competition. Even though the big distributors do a good job of meeting all the buyer's commodity needs," he explained, "many specialty suppliers will always prefer to sell direct through a supplier-neutral channel like SciQuest. Plus we are a technology company. They are not."

In fact, SciQuest has had only one real competitor: Chemdex, a subsidiary of Ventro Corporation. But after a series of disappointing revenue gains, Chemdex announced in November 2000, that it was closing its Web operation. Its mistake, Andrews believes, was focusing too much on pleasing buyers while neglecting the needs of the major direct suppliers. When the big manufacturers refused to sign up for Chemdex's online catalog, customers opted for the one-stop shopping at SciQuest.

It's comparatively easy to sign up small suppliers for its electronic catalog, according to Andrews, though it took some pampering. Many need help in setting up and managing an electronic catalog, and SciQuest had to make sure they didn't have exaggerated expectations about floods of revenue from the Internet.

The major suppliers have been slower to sign up. For one thing, their marketing expenses are lower than those of the small shops, and their brands are strong enough that they don't need more exposure. But they were worth much more to SciQuest than their smaller counterparts. It takes just as much work to add a small supplier to the list as it takes to catalog a much more extensive line. As a practical matter for a start-up operation, Andrews needed to fatten his catalog with some big brand leaders before spending money to add hundreds of small ones. Perhaps most important, as the fate of Chemdex proved, the big suppliers are essential in attracting SciQuest's ultimate customer.

Andrews's first approach to the major producers was the familiar argument of the Internet entrepreneur: "If you don't participate, you're risking not being a leader in developing this new channel, which will have a huge impact on your long-term profitability."

But SciQuest's major lure for the big producers was a class system that recognized that some suppliers were more equal than others. The big ones, said Andrews, have strong brands that have earned the large profit margins that cover their high infrastructure costs. They don't want to be dumped into a price-driven Wal-Mart atmosphere.

"No big supplier wants to come onto a level playing field," he told me. "They see that as unfair. They have better understood customers' needs, they have delivered better products and better service, and they have earned dominant market share the hard way." Acknowledging that, SciQuest enables its customers to position and promote key suppliers in users' search results. The small niche supplier might want "preferred positioning" too, but that is between them and the customer.

This approach benefits buyers, too, Andrews argues: "Let's say I'm looking for microscopes. I really don't want to compare 50,000 products from 50 suppliers. Let me see the market leaders' products first, because I know they have a proven reputation. If I don't find what I want, I can scan down the results and see the rest of the world. That's the quickest, easiest shopping experience I can get."

SciQuest says more than two-thirds of the largest suppliers in the scientific marketplace are participating in its customers' private marketplaces. It has also signed up buyers such as Du Pont Pharmaceutical and Memorial Sloan-Kettering to operate on tailored versions of SciQuest's systems and processes that mesh seamlessly with their own procurement, financial, and research operations. "We have marquee customers and marquee suppliers," explained Andrews. "In making markets, it's the chicken and the egg."

SciQuest, like most e-enterprises, has yet to make a profit—and the millennial message from Wall Street has prompted it to rethink parts of its business model, focusing on earnings instead of revenue growth. Andrews told me that SciQuest hoped to reach the break-even point in the third quarter of 2002. If that happens, Wall Street may finally recognize what SciQuest has accomplished. Let me set down some of the business principles Scott Andrews has followed; they echo many of the bedrock ideas behind X-engineering.

- Start with a great aspiration—reinventing a whole industry, for example.

- Be persistent. Harmonizing processes across organizations is not easy, and adoption time may take longer than you expected, and your business direction may take unexpected turns.

- Fragmented industries provide a great opportunity for consolidators, companies that offer customers great choice combined with ease of search and purchase.

- Start slowly with a simple proposition, then build on that proposition as you get market traction—but be prepared to adjust that proposition based on what customer pull is telling you.

- Use process excellence as a differentiator. Unique processes can be the proposition that you offer your customers.

- Share your unique differentiator processes only with your customers. Otherwise, be open with your processes and share your good ideas broadly.

- Develop common or standard information technology platforms so you can operate easily across organizations. The platforms will represent an important business asset.

- Create trust to cement your relationships with partners and assure their participation in your proposition.

- Live by your understanding of customer pull and process push. It can enable you to build a company that has virtual scale as large as an industry.

This chapter has described SciQuest in detail so that you might learn from what Scott Andrews has done right as he created a new business. The next chapter examines a different kind of organization—a venerable bank with a long history that is working to reinvent itself. Both provide lessons that will apply to your own X-engineering efforts.

Chapter 12

X-Engineering in Action—PNC Bank

You might expect that industries that specialize in providing information would be the first to embrace the changes made possible by advances in information technology in general and the Internet in particular. But that isn't always the case. Information is unquestionably a core element of the service and products in the financial-services industry; further, the financial-services industry is one for which the label "e-commerce" actually has an authentic ring. Yet traditional banks have been surprisingly slow to change and adapt their processes to new technologies.

In the earlier chapters of this book I suggested why some companies might be slow to move, including their fear of the unknown, their refusal to face reality, their arrogance, and the "not-on-my-watch" syndrome. Most banking organizations have been guilty of one or more of those sins.

In this chapter I introduce you to an exception: PNC, a company that lives by the principles of X-engineering. There are several noteworthy qualities in its work: the aspiration of its managers, the scale of its mobilization, the breadth of its opportunity pursuit, and the skills and knowledge with which it is implementing its strategies. PNC is leading a campaign that will never end. This case is a work in progress.

I invite you to pay special attention to the description of the "brainstorming" session that was held within PNC Bank, PNC's largest business unit. It begins with a discussion of how electronic signatures might change some of the bank's processes. The discussion illustrates how one idea builds on another. It is a good example of the inductive thinking that X-engineering requires. That is, given a new technological development, how can you make the most of it in your business? The discussion also shows that good ideas generally don't arrive as a bolt from the blue; they come as the result of the hard intellectual work that managers too often neglect.

A Perfectly Upbeat Bank

Tim Shack is a savvy business and technology leader who has spent 23 years perfecting the processes and systems at Pennsylvania-based PNC Bank Corporation. Now PNC's chief information officer, Shack describes the Internet's impact on PNC as a "thousand-percent revolution." This is "fundamentally changing the way we do business, both externally and internally," he told me. "This is not just about technology, but about reinvention—how you must X-engineer inside and out, how you and your competitors must change. Why? Because the customer is in charge of all the decision making." That's right, Shack repeats: The customer now literally runs PNC. "I've never seen anything like it in my entire career."

Because PNC sees the new world so clearly—and because everyone, top to bottom, agrees on the need to adjust to that world—the bank is an outstanding example of X-engineering in action. In this chapter we will see in detail exactly how and why PNC has followed the X-engineering route to grow where the potential is biggest. Says the new chief executive officer, Jim Rohr, "We're leveraging one of the industry's best technological platforms to become a leader in e-commerce."

In recent years, PNC has transformed itself from a traditional regional bank to a diversified financial-services company. Beginning as Pittsburgh National Bank with its roots in the steel industry, it grew through a series of mergers into a five-state power, operating in Pennsylvania, New Jersey, Delaware, Ohio, and Kentucky. But the traditional banking business is now just 55 percent of PNC's $5.2 billion in annual revenues; the rest comes from seven other money-centered businesses, ranging from corporate banking and real-estate finance to wealth management, asset management, and mutual-fund processing. PNC has also jointly invested in new ventures with partners to help acquire capabilities beyond its experience in finance. Several of these ventures are being built on the bank's technology platform.

PNC's seven businesses are organized as separate companies within the PNC framework, which itself is managed by a small corporate staff. The structure is designed to allow each enterprise to focus on its own customers and its own area of the financial world, and thus to compete successfully with small companies springing up in each field. Impressed by the result, other banks have begun to follow PNC's lead.

Each business is run by its own chief executive, who controls its budgeting and resource allocation. The central corporate staff furnishes services such as shared technology, marketing, and legal help. But it also provides crucial guidance and leadership in the X-engineering of all the divisions. The idea, Tim Shack says, is "to have these independently managed businesses not only compete with their best-of-class competitors, but also to exploit the leverage opportunities within the company by bringing the total PNC together with focus on the customer. Now the whole is greater than the sum of its parts." The office of the chairman functions as a kind of strategic investor or portfolio manager, overseeing the seven businesses, deciding where to invest more money, and nudging strategy decisions to encourage synergy, cross-selling, and long-range coherence.

All told, Shack explained, PNC is a model remarkably well suited to e-commerce because the company has decided to X-engineer all the processes of its businesses, sharpening their competitive edge in the Internet world.

As he described it, the plan calls for PNC to create seven e-businesses, whose respective processes will interact more and more, forming collective processes and eventually a Net-based powerhouse in e-commerce. "In financial services, nobody can afford to ignore e-commerce anymore," Shack maintains. "It's no longer an alternative. It's the core of every business."

When PNC bet its future on X-engineering, three prerequisites for success were in place. First, PNC's management had stayed informed about key developments in financial services and technology. They were realistic about their markets and their own capabilities. Second, CEO Jim Rohr and his colleagues were poised to make whatever radical changes PNC needed to outperform its competitors. They had an appetite for change and were prepared to move. And third, while they agreed on specific steps ahead, they were prepared to adapt to whatever new directions their experience dictated. On the road to transformation they would be nimble and not try to pre-plan every step.

From the corporate viewpoint, PNC had three strategic goals:

1. To enhance value for its customers by creating a multi-channel, integrated customer Web experience

2. To lead the financial-services industry in creating a completely new standard of operating efficiency made possible by e-commerce

3. To continue its own evolution from the capital-intensive traditional banking business into higher-valued processing businesses driven by fee income and e-business.

To make all this happen, PNC set up a new unit called TechWork@PNC, a kind of internal consulting firm and catalyst assigned to addressing and speeding up the X-engineering process. Headed by Tom Kunz, who reports to Shack, TechWork coordinates strategy, researches problems, ensures a common technology platform, and generally helps to incubate changes after everyone agrees they are needed. Located in a high-tech environment, TechWork develops ideas and processes that move directly into the seven business operations.

As X-engineering began, PNC's seven businesses were at widely divergent stages of e-commerce. The retail banking operation was most advanced, with a Web site that enabled customers to make transactions as well as get information. In addition, PNC's joint venture projects included the joint PNC–Perot Systems investment in a company called BillingZone that aims to be a major player in business-to-business electronic bill payment. At the other extreme, PNC's corporate banking and real-estate finance businesses had Web sites that were at the early stages of providing information and enabling customer transactions.

Given all these disparate pieces of the PNC pie, Kunz's assignment from Shack was to devise a strategic plan for steering all PNC businesses in a cohesive direction, driven by the diverse customer segments it serves, PNC was to respond to customer pull.

That wasn't easy: Conditions were very different in each business. For example, retail e-banking was problematic. According to Kunz, the field was "littered" with e-services that made customers happy but failed to make money. In the early euphoria of e-commerce, that didn't trouble investors, but now it bothered CEO Rohr and his colleagues. The new skepticism meant that Joe Guyaux, chief executive of the retail banking business, would have to be even more careful in choosing services to provide. By contrast, business-to-business banking was relatively undeveloped, with few precedents to provide guidance for PNC's managers. Much customer contact and market research were needed to determine not only what the customers wanted, but what they could use and would pay for.

Shack and Kunz had an acute sense of the pitfalls lurking in e-commerce. For one thing, as Kunz warned his chief executive clients, you can spend a lot of money on X-engineering without creating value; choices must be sharply focused. For another, it takes more time, energy, and commitment than anyone expects to create a first-class Internet experience for customers. And finally, X-engineering requires a whole new approach to doing business in terms of skills, speed, and technology.

The Search for New X-Engineers

One big problem was how to get PNC's workforce up to speed for life in the new Internet world. Each business would need a steady infusion of Generation X and Generation Y staffers who were already information-technology-savvy. That meant recruiting people who had been more attracted to technology companies than to the staid world of banking. Meanwhile, PNC's current executives had to become what Kunz calls "Web-savvy"—if not totally proficient, at least comfortably familiar with Internet language and capabilities. All this required careful recruiting, constant education, and lots of attention, all of it tailored specifically to each of the seven businesses.

PNC now begins scouting bright people even before they get out of high school. In partnership with the University of Pittsburgh, Penn State University, and Carnegie Mellon, the bank runs a yearly talent search for the top 50 technology-oriented high-school juniors in Pennsylvania. During the summer before they become seniors, the students get special courses, including pep talks by PNC executives on the bank's problems and prospects. The aim, says Kunz, is to make these young people see financial services as cool stuff for smart people to work on.

The bank's talent hunt continues right through graduate school. PNC is one of several companies sponsoring Carnegie Mellon's leading master of science and e-commerce program, in which PNC executives actually teach classes—and from which they hire graduates for the bank's X-engineering effort.

PNC lost a few top people in the rush to dot-com start-ups in 1999 and early 2000, but the subsequent Internet stock crash helped stem that drain, and in any case, says Kunz, "Money is just one of the motivators. We have been able to keep a lot of good people that you might have expected to be lured away."

From Technology to Process

The technological challenges of X-engineering at PNC are formidable. For one thing, the Web experience for customers of the seven businesses must be not only unique to each enterprise, but also compatible with PNC's overall systems and processes. The right content must be delivered seamlessly in a user-sensitive way. And PNC is digitally daring: It envisions its future Web pages as far more flexible than most, virtually created by customers according to their wants rather than dictated by the bank's purposes.

As Kunz sees it, e-commerce is nothing like a playing field for Gen-X gaming and gossiping. This is grown-up business, he says, a tool for pragmatic executives to wring every ounce of creativity and efficiency out of myriad business processes. Most important, e-business must support the overall strategy of each business. Sites must be designed accordingly. They must be friendly to first-time users—fast at providing information, simple in handling purchases, easy for novices to navigate while seeking a certain page or, most important, returning to it next time. At another extreme, PNC sites must work flawlessly for regular users who want to integrate relevant portions into their own desktops. These users require processes they can totally rely on, a degree of process harmonization that I described as mutuality. E-banking is one industry that cannot afford product recalls.

As I write, all of PNC's seven businesses have advanced their online processes to offer sophisticated access to customer information, allowing customers to perform transactions. In effect, they are climbing a ladder of increasing complexity in terms of process and technology. The ladder begins with the X-engineering of the process that gives customers access to their own accounts—aggregated across the company, with a single sign-on. Next comes the customer self-service process, enabling online inquiries and requests about individual accounts. At a higher level, Kunz and company are X-engineering the process of self-banking, allowing people to open new accounts and make purchases online.

Many of these initiatives focus on retail customers and small-to-medium-sized businesses. But PNC is also reaching out to larger commercial customers. One example is BillingZone, a PNC venture that handles electronic billing and payments between businesses. This Web-based enterprise may sound like simple out-sourcing, but the service is actually quite sophisticated. It requires a deep understanding of how companies create and pay invoices and how to harmonize those processes across organizational boundaries. To do this, PNC has leaned heavily on its experience in providing treasury services to commercial customers. PNC is a leading treasury management provider to more than 30,000 customers, many of whom could benefit from the process consolidation that BillingZone offers. Companies such as Procter and Gamble and Xerox—giant billers—have already signed up for BillingZone's services.

In each case, the services are painstakingly designed to avoid any radical changes in the workflow or existing systems of customers, be they the bill presenters or the bill payers. BillingZone takes all the information a biller, for example, uses to present a bill, and translates it so that the biller need not make any additional technology investment. By the same token, the payer simply signs on to BillingZone and sets up its hierarchies and bank accounts and is then ready to start receiving bills. In that sense, BillingZone is an intermediary that, in X-engineering terms, provides harmonizing processes.

BillingZone's proposition goes far beyond that of the traditional outsourcing operation, which is limited to reducing costs and inefficiencies. It completes transactions more rapidly, and it allows for a closeness between biller and payer that eliminates many sources of friction.

Let's suppose we are back in the paper world. You have ordered five Xerox machine parts from your supplier, but only four have arrived. You are not happy, and doubly so when you look at the bill requesting payment for five. You send off a check for the four items, and make a phone call complaining about not receiving the fifth item you need. Your check arrives a week or two later, and then starts the familiar exchange of faxes and telephonic discussions as to what went wrong and why.

Now, let's move to the world of BillingZone. You sign on to the Web site, and there's the invoice from your supplier, asking for payment for four items. You leave a message for the supplier on the site, explaining what's happened. As a result, the supplier discovers the problem before any payment is made and within a matter of hours or days, not weeks. That gives the supplier a chance to immediately correct the billing error. Beyond that, it enables the supplier to deliver the fifth item.

From your point of view, the confusion is cleared up far faster than is typical in the paper world. The potential of the incident for damaging your relationship with the supplier is defused. That's good news for the supplier, who is also happy to be able to move quickly to repair any weaknesses in its delivery system.

Francine Miltenberger, head of PNC's Treasury Management group, sees other advantages in X-engineering. For one, the company is ahead of the pack: PNC's focus on the Internet puts it in the avant-garde of the digital age. For another, "We realize that fully 80 percent of things our clients are calling us for we could convert to self-help on the Web and make it easier on us to provide a higher level of service." Example: Almost 4,000 of PNC's commercial customers now use the bank's Internet service center to answer their service questions.

The company's technological leadership has also yielded an unexpected side benefit. When the company began its Web operations, their value was measured in terms of the number of customers using the online service. That measure has proven inadequate. Research has shown that most of PNC's customers who use online services stay with the bank longer and buy more services than non-users.

The Power of the Three Ps

As the players tell it, X-engineering at PNC is hard work. But Kunz says his goal is to make it so ingrained in the corporate fabric that people constantly think about it. He meets frequently with the CEO, business segment heads, and attends any other meetings that touch on e-commerce.

One of the benefits and challenges of these meetings is that, in addition to discussing the role of e-business in advancing customer strategies, they inevitably encompass all three legs of the X-engineering triangle. A discussion of process, for example, sparks fresh ideas as to a new and improved business proposition, which, in turn, produces ideas for increasing the participation of more players in the X-engineering program. So it turns out that X-engineering itself is a process—a heuristic process of one discovery spawning another in an endless cycle.

The focus of one PNC brainstorming session not long ago was on leveraging the process of gathering e-mail addresses and allowing e-signatures at the retail bank, whose customers include both consumers and small-to-medium-sized businesses.

Recent federal legislation allows documents in many transactions to be signed and acknowledged electronically rather than signed by the parties in person and approved by bank personnel. For banks and other organizations swimming in paperwork, this could mean substantial savings. So the PNC session was called to identify not only immediate benefits but also opportunities for long-term payoffs from electronic signature processes. About 12 people attended the meeting, representing various operational parts of the retail bank and the bank's information-technology organization. The discussion progressed through the Three Ps, touching in turn on process, proposition, and participation as the group groped for ways to move beyond incremental improvements to real X-engineering breakthroughs.

PROCESSES

The discussion began with some brainstorming about new business possibilities that e-signatures opened up. For example, it was pointed out that the bank could seek new customers in quite remote locations. Those customers had previously needed several pieces of executed paper to open an account. Now they could do it with just an e-signature. It would also be possible to execute loan agreements remotely, without exchanging cumbersome documents, and so the bank could pursue more borrowers over a much wider area.

The brainstormers came up with many such ideas. But after the first hour, it became increasingly clear that the advantages of the e-signature would be merely incremental, adding revenues in processes that were already well established. Unless the bank took an even broader look at its retail operations, no real breakthroughs were likely.

So the team tabled its first set of ideas and moved to a second discussion. This one began by listing the retail bank's major processes and what each one cost to perform. One team member described the work of Genesis, a project aimed at reengineering the retail bank's operations and computer systems. He described all the new customer services and operating efficiencies that Genesis promised. But as the group talked about how e-signatures and other new electronic processes could further enhance the retail bank's efficiency, it became clear for the second time that these benefits were also likely to be merely incremental.

The team was quickly proving to itself that nothing truly significant would change in the retail bank's operational performance unless an even more ambitious objective could be established. Jim Rohr had been encouraging his managers to be aggressively aspirational in what they wanted to achieve. It was becoming clear to this team that if they wanted to do real reinvention in retail banking they'd have to take Rohr's advice.

PROPOSITION

Then one team member suggested that it would be a great strategic advantage if the bank could significantly grow its checking account or FDIC insured deposit business by providing further value-added services.

Other team members suggested two new areas for development that could contribute to customer acquisition and retention. The first proposal was that the retail bank find some means to act as an aggregator of customer information. After all, one person pointed out, customers shopping for banks are looking for services to help them track money, spend money, and save money. Right now, the financial-services industry assumes that people want to do business with a single institution. But few customers behave that way. Most deal with a patchwork of financial vehicles—insurance companies, mutual funds, and brokerage houses as well as banks. Most people cannot begin to tell you how well their total assets are performing today, much less reconcile their current net worth.

What if the bank could act as an aggregator? Customers consider their bank to be their primary financial provider. Its X-engineered service would provide every retail customer with regular statements of all his or her assets, no matter where they were located.

Someone piped up, "This would allow us to provide the same kind of service to every retail customer that we provide to our private-banking clients." Someone added, "That should be our aspiration." Someone else added, "But we must do it at a very low transaction cost."

At this point, the team was entering the realm of reinvention. The notion that PNC could give retail customers regular information on all their assets was a breakthrough fulfillment of the company's service proposition, making customers' lives simpler.

That was not, however, the end of the team's inventiveness.

213

"Can we find a way to crack another major customer need—the ability to pay bills simply and efficiently?" someone asked. After all, the bank already knows the customer's payment schedule because it processes his or her checks every month. If the customer approved, the bank could easily use this information to X-engineer an automatic system for paying all regular bills. Eureka! Customers could finally quit writing and mailing those monthly checks and tediously balancing their checkbooks. Hidden bank hands would take care of everything. It was yet another idea that fulfilled the service proposition and could win new customers for PNC.

By the end of the session, the team had identified three good ways to boost the bank's retail business—acquiring new customers, providing current financial data, paying bills electronically. All these processes were subject to X-engineered improvements, using Internet technology. All supported the company's service business proposition of simplifying their customers' lives.

Participation

Back the team went to discuss some banking basics. One person pointed to the heart of retail banking—the checking accounts that largely make up a retail bank's customer base. Any significant loss of checking-account customers is bad news for the bank. How could PNC not only retain but multiply such customers? The right answer would do wonders for growing the business.

Soon the team's conversation focused on what happens when retail banks go after their competitors' customers. Remember when banks offered incentives like freebie toasters to get people to switch? That would be laughable today. People need a lot more than toasters as an incentive to change banks. What's more, even if a bank offers something smarter—notably better fees and interest rates—the process of switching accounts typically confronts the customer with hassles that seem absurd in the digital age. The wait for outstanding checks, the transfer of automatic payments, the time needed to close out an account, the paperwork to open a new account—such bureaucratic irritations seem designed to discourage bank customers from moving elsewhere. Even if your friendly bank treats you badly, it's often easier to stay put.

The team went to work on X-engineering the customer acquisition process. For example, what if the bank could use the Internet to acquire all necessary account-switching information about potential customers in advance? Even before the customer decided to switch, the bank's computers would be ready to fill out all those infernal forms automatically. The bank would retrieve outstanding checks from the customer's former bank and take over automatic payments. There would be no overlapping accounts to allow checks to clear, no need to deal with utilities to switch payment systems—no hassle at all. The customer would merely have to submit one approval signature, either in writing or electronically. Presto: The customer would have a new bank as painlessly as pressing "Enter" on his or her keyboard.

Such a move would revolutionize the whole customer acquisition process. It would allow PNC Bank to compete on the basis of real service and real products, leaping ahead of an industry that retains thousands of customers only because it makes it so hard for them to switch their business. If PNC could penetrate that vast pool of dissatisfaction, it would win new accounts by the truckload.

A fly on the wall at these breakthrough discussions would have noticed that X-engineering is not only a heuristic process, but that the resulting discoveries have a common trait. They all seem to open up the playing field and the number and variety of players. They are inclusive rather than exclusive. In PNC's case, this particular discussion began with the bank as institution, expanded to the bank's people and processes at all levels, rapidly encompassed the customers with all their specific frustrations, and ultimately conceived a new banker-customer partnership of huge potential benefit to all parties.

As the team stepped back and contemplated its discussion, it recognized that it had taken a long journey in a mere two hours. It had begun with a focus on using e-signatures to make the bank more cost-efficient, then progressed to using e-signatures to expand the bank's customer base, and from there climbed to new high ground. It was clear from these examples that the greatest opportunities would come from X-engineering all the bank's processes to maximum efficiency, using online technology, and then from combining these enhancements in ways that created new value propositions for its customers.

Another realization: The team was now thinking about the Internet as a marketing tool. The more information it could gather effectively about its customers and its potential customers, the more it could directly offer them value-added services.

There has been some debate as to whether the next round of benefit from the Internet would come from a focus on go-to-market processes (marketing, sales, distribution) or whether it would come from reengineering a company's supply chain. I see that debate as academic.

The next round of the Internet's benefit will come both from making customer-facing processes more productive and from streamlining and harmonizing all types of processes and relationships within and between companies. This PNC X-engineering team had just come to the same conclusion. It recognized that the new Genesis system, which operates the retail bank's infrastructure, could be dramatically leveraged. The key was to connect Genesis to new technology-enabled ways of going to market. Aspiration had done its work in helping the team develop insight. Now the job of more detailed design lay ahead.

The Take-off Platform

In all major X-engineering decisions, the strategic aspiration takes the lead in setting priorities and measuring opportunities against what customers want, what competitors are doing, and PNC's own goals. The point, says Tim Shack, is to stretch the organization's thinking, make sure strategies mesh, and advance the common technological platform.

In several cases, PNC's individual businesses have proposed systems that would not fit the platform. If they can show that their approach makes a real difference to their customers and thus helps generate profits, Shack and Kunz are prepared to go along and find ways to integrate the new technology. But in most cases, Shack says, it makes no real difference to the customer, and "We're able to demonstrate that using the shared infrastructure results in more rapid time-to-market with lower costs." After that, the business CEOs have no problem going along.

Timing is a major factor in coordinating X-engineering: One of the businesses may be ready to make a move ahead of the rest, but its decision can't be made without taking the needs of others into consideration. Not long ago, for instance, the strategy group worked out a policy on how all the PNC Web sites should handle technology for the process known as customer relationship management. "The goal is to give all customers a common experience with PNC wherever they touch us," Shack told me. "We came together to select the solution platform, and agreed collectively across businesses that we would implement one technology." As successive PNC enterprises develop their customer relationship programs, they will follow the corporate example.

Shack emphasizes that all big organizations have to focus their bets: "You can't be everything to everybody, and a company our size has to be very good at what it does if it doesn't want to make a $100 million mistake." PNC's original big bet was that

"Bringing all these disparate banks and businesses together on a common technology platform is a key ingredient in being successful over the long haul." One measure of the payoff in the investment in e-business technologies came early in 2000, when PNC beat all estimates on the cost of combating the Y2K bogey and spent just a fraction of what comparable banks had to pay. Another measure is that competitors are abandoning their own costly bets—on stand-alone e-business units, spinning off businesses, or buying links to major portals—and instead are beginning to imitate the PNC model.

If a bet is focused and doesn't put the whole business at risk, Shack says, failure won't be catastrophic—and may even be beneficial. For example, PNC put a lot of money into trying to grow its credit-card business, only to discover that it required a much greater scale than the company could handle. "We ended up selling that business," says Shack. "The good side was that it forced us to develop consumer-lending capabilities that we have now used to become the home equity consumer lending provider for American Express, Prudential, and NetBank. We were able to leverage a setback and create a whole new business. Even the bad bet paid off."

By 2002, Kunz predicts, all PNC's businesses will be X-engineered and fully Internet-enabled. "It will be a much more efficient organization," he says, "one whose business mix has improved, with new businesses sprouting from the growth of e-commerce. From the customer's perspective, it's easy to do business. For the shareholder, it creates more value. And for the employee—well, I'm working for a company that is one of the leaders of the digital age."

But X-engineering won't stop there. PNC simply assumes that technology never stops advancing and will enable the bank to do more and more process change. Wireless technologies are probably next, says Shack, and will doubtless change the financial-services world again in ways that are hard to predict. His job is to make sure that PNC never stops trying to anticipate those changes. The mandates: Stay close to your customers. Think big. Dream up new directions. Jump aboard others' innovations whenever necessary. Just don't sit and wait: "You don't want to wake up one day when other organizations have jumped on that next disruptive technology, and you haven't yet done anything about it."

This spirit has led one banking analyst to describe PNC as "one of the smartest banks around." It has become a leader in applying technology to solving customers' problems in ways that create new value. It was recently recognized by *Internet Week* as one of the top 100 e-businesses and was the leading bank in *Information Week*'s 500 Report for 2001. PNC has joined the ranks of some impressive pioneers, including Solectron, EMC, and Dell. These companies all demonstrate that successful X-engineering begins with the drive of creative leaders and goes on from there to link companies in profitable alliances that can ultimately transform entire industries.

Epilogue

The last half of the twentieth century was a fertile time for deep thoughts on how to manage business. It got underway with Peter Drucker's landmark book, *Management*, which offered advice for professionalizing the managerial function. The spotlight then shifted to strategy, and companies came to be defined by their products and markets.

In the next stage, leading management thinkers, Drucker included, focused on the customer. A company, they said, should be defined by the needs, values, and expectations of their customers. Other strategists said the emphasis belonged on a company's competencies, while Mike Hammer and I emphasized the importance of processes.

When we introduced the concept of reengineering ten years ago, we highlighted key words in its definition. Those words were *fundamental, radical, dramatic,* and *process.* The first three words were intended to describe the degree of change and the business result that reengineering would produce. The fourth word, *process,* was reengineering's focus.

As you have seen in this book, X-engineering emphasizes much of the same, but it goes further. Its definition adds the key words *technology-enabled, connect, efficiency,* and *value for customers.* Processes in X-engineering will be dramatically affected by technology. Connectivity between companies and their customers is at X-engineering's core. And while the principal benefit for many companies may be efficiency, X-engineering should be practiced with a view toward creating value for customers.

In this book I have also gone further than we did in reengineering and argued that a company is actually defined by its processes. I have argued that X-engineering holds great promise for dramatically improving not only the performance of companies but the efficiency of whole industries. My hope is that I have made my case and that you will put these ideas into practice.

I should make it clear, however, that I view X-engineering as something more than management process or a set of ideas. It is the key to opening an entirely new place for the conduct of business—what some have called the networked economy. You might say that place is the fourth *P* in X-engineering, together with process, proposition, and participation.

I recognize that this place will not be built easily, that many companies may be slow in adopting the practices I espouse in this book. But I have no doubt that companies and industries will eventually begin to operate as I have described. Competitive forces are too strong, inefficiencies too great, and information technology too potent to allow otherwise. For business in general, that transformation could take as long as a decade.

But you would do well to make your move sooner. Your partners and customers are waiting for you to bring them the benefits of the new business world that X-engineering makes possible, but their patience is not unlimited.

And what does this new world, this new place of business, look like?

It is a place where companies run so well and so consistently that their performance is predictable and constantly improving.

It is a place where a company's knowledge is highly valued but openly shared.

It is a place where simplicity has replaced complexity and redundant work has disappeared.

It is a place where innovation is nurtured by a constant and ubiquitous flow of information supported by an invisible technology infrastructure.

It is a place where managers know what is unique to their company and are prepared to let go of the rest.

It is a place where companies and customers work together in harmony, where trust is built on an in-depth understanding of each other's business.

It is a place where companies are distinguished by their ability to execute.

It is a place where information technology supports and improves the human potential and where there is pride and dignity in work.

That is the place where X-engineering can take you. Have a great journey.

Acknowledgments

This is the fifth book that I have either authored, co-authored, or edited. I began each project with great optimism, always forgetting how much real work it takes to research and write a book. But I never forget all the people who have helped—with inspiration, ideas, research, editing, and just plain encouragement.

On this project, I was particularly inspired by a group of managers, many of whom agreed to have the stories of their companies serve as examples of X-engineering. They are building great companies, and I am privileged to have them as friends. They include Bud Mathaisel of Solectron, Charlie Baker of Harvard Pilgrim Health Care, Richard Keyser of W. W. Grainger, Gil Minor of Owens & Minor, Scott Andrews of SciQuest, Mike Ruettgers of EMC, and Jim Rohr of PNC Bank. I thank them and all the other managers whose work and ideas provided the basis for this book.

As with my previous books, I am also indebted to the talented people at Wordworks, Inc.—Donna Sammons Carpenter, Maurice

Acknowledgments

Coyle, Toni Porcelli, Cindy Sammons, and Robert W. Stock. They would have never stopped working on this book if my publisher hadn't demanded the manuscript.

On the subject of my publisher, I thank Larry Kirshbaum of Time Warner for seeing the merits of this project well before it was fully conceived. At Time Warner, the project would not have seen its way to completion without the constant support of my editor, Zach Schisgal. Thanks, Zach, for all your wisdom and for staying with it. Helen Rees, my agent, did her normal wonderful job of helping all along the way, as did Barbara Hendra in the publicity for this book.

I have always benefited from having great colleagues in my consulting work, many of whom have contributed their insights and experiences to this book. They include Jack Calhoun, Lou Pahountis, Bob Suh, and Tom Roloff. I also want to thank Ross Perot, Jr., for believing in this book and his support for the project.

While I was writing this book, I had the opportunity to work with Jim Ware and Steve Stanton of the Concours Group on a related research project. It was a great help to discuss my ideas with Jim, Steve, their colleagues, and their clients. It gave me another window into what was happening in business and to judge the Internet's effects.

But my closest supporters, critics, and collaborators have always been my wife, Lois, and my son, Adam. They unselfishly give me the time to write and then anxiously read what I have written. Their insights show up in many ways in this book.

And, of course, I must thank you, the reader. It is only through your work that these ideas will have value.

Index

Index